VICTIMS

NO MORE!

Fighting Back Against
An Active Shooter

DAVE ACOSTA

DAVE ACOSTA

DEDICATION

I dedicate this book to the brave men and women behind the badge—those who run into the gunfight without hesitation.

I also dedicate this book to those, who at their own peril, choose to Fight Back on behalf of others. People like James Shaw, Riley Howell, Kendrick Castillo, Joshua Quick and so many others who have mounted a counter-attack against the cowards who massacre innocent people, and take them down. Their actions have saved countless lives, sometimes at the expense of their own.

I can't mention selfless acts of courage without including countless educators who are not only willing to love and teach our children daily, but who are willing to protect them, on our behalf, with their very lives if necessary.

Above all, I dedicate this book to the incredible men and women of United Flight 93, who on September 11th, 2001, stood up and fought back in the face of evil and won. Through their choice to fight back they saved more lives than we will ever know, and so doing changed our culture forever. Their example of selfless sacrifice proved that even unarmed people, if united and determined, can defeat armed terrorists. Hijacking a plane in U.S. airspace will never be productive again, because Americans decided together, in that very moment, that it would never again be a viable option.

CONTENTS

INTRODUCTION

Refuse to be a victim.

Victims have no options.

At 8:46 a.m. on the morning of September 11, 2001, a commercial airliner hit the World Trade Center North Tower in New York City. America watched, wondering what had happened.

At 9:03 a.m. a second plane crashed into the South Tower, and everyone suddenly understood we were under attack—and no one knew how many more there would be, or the extent of the attacks. **We were scared.**

We felt powerless to protect ourselves. The best we could do was wait to see what else the enemy would throw at us.

At 9:37 a.m. hijackers aboard Flight 77 crashed the plane into the Pentagon in Arlington County, Virginia. **We felt defenseless, unable to stop the attack.**

At 9:59 a.m. the South Tower of the World Trade Center collapsed. **We felt vulnerable, without any ability to help ourselves or stop the pain.**

Friends and relatives on the ground informed passengers and crewmembers aboard hijacked Flight 93 about the attacks in New York and Washington. At that point the passengers made a crucial decision. **They would no longer**

be helpless. They would not stand by and allow hijackers to crash their plane into a building filled with fellow Americans. Although none of them were air marshals or police, they took back control, and mounted an attempt to retake the plane, forcing the hijackers to relinquish control, one way or another. *As of that moment, in the sky over Pennsylvania, we were no longer a nation of victims.*

Since that day each attempt to hijack an American airplane has been met with a counter-attack by the passengers on board. I don't care what weapon you have in your hand, you will not kick in a cockpit door on an airplane again! We will tackle you, fight you and crush the life out of you with our bare hands before we let you crash another airplane into any building in the United States. As a society we have taken responsibility for our own safety in the air.

> *The attempt to hijack airplanes to use as weapons against Americans has become unproductive, and is no longer an option for terrorists, because Americans are no longer victims in the sky.*

As I stood among the survivors just after the Sutherland Springs First Baptist Church mass shootings, the bodies still on the floor and slumped in the pews where they fell, a distraught young female television news reporter came up to me and asked, "Mr. Acosta, when will this insanity end?"

I looked at her and said, "Mass shootings will stop in this country when they are no longer productive."

Prepare to be the solution.

ACKNOWLEDGMENTS

I'd like to thank my wife Danielle, who has supported and encouraged me to push forward with Fight Back Nation. She has been to every training session and has seen first-hand the transformation of over 7,000 educators from potential victim, to capable and confident protector. She has been by my side every step of the way.

I read the book, *Terror at Beslan: A Russian Tragedy with Lessons for America's Schools*, by Dr. John Giduck. It chronicled the events of the world's worst school shooting. John pleaded for us to be vigilant, to acknowledge that something like this can happen here in the US. It inspired me to work hard to find a solution that would save lives. Thank you John for your dedication and commitment to continuous education on matters of terrorism and for encouraging me to charge forward in my endeavor to empower others.

I went to a local charter school, American Leadership Academy (ALA), and pitched my idea to the director, Kenna Vallejos. She embraced the program and introduced me to an administrator, Shad Stevens, who agreed. I can't thank Kenna and Shad enough for helping me prove my training program with these amazing educators.

I'm grateful for the professional and personal relationship I've developed with American Preparatory Academy administrator Tim Evancich. He too embraced the program and made the training mandatory for all APA staff. He has been a huge contributor to the evolution of the program and been an incredible champion and advocate for Fight Back Nation in the charter school community.

Juab School District Superintendent Rick Robins also stepped up and embraced the program and put all of his staff through the training as well. His was the first complete school district in the US to have all schools designated as Fight Back Nation certified schools. I am grateful to Rick for pushing past external skepticism and giving me the opportunity to show him what his teachers were capable of. They are truly the epitome of a Fight Back culture.

In a Nutshell

My name is Dave Acosta, and I'm the founder of Fight Back Nation. I also train international SWAT Teams, presidential security details, close protection units, and have dedicated my life to training schools, governments, corporations and other organizations how to protect against active and mass shooters.

The methods I teach in schools and offices are simple and effective. Anyone can learn to defend against an active shooter, and disarm him if he's close enough. The concepts and techniques I am sharing with you in this book are the same concepts and techniques I teach with my team in conferences and training sessions around the nation and the world.

You can view short demonstration videos on our website at FightBackNation.org/video to help you visualize and implement what we are discussing here.

My team and I have trained thousands of schoolteachers and others to use these concepts and techniques. I've seen many of them transformed from scared, crying and shaking at the very thought of an active shooter, to fully empowered and confident in their ability to fight back and win against an active shooter. I have watched proudly as timid 110-pound teachers disarm and even accidentally injure my capable, fit, experienced volunteers and instructors as they learn and practice our simple disarming technique.

This book is a crash course in successfully defending against the harsh and cruel reality of an ultraviolent encounter. I present the truth of things as they really are. I am not politically motivated or politically correct—most mass shooters are men, and most schoolteachers are women—so I will use gender specific pronouns like *he* and *she*, even if it is generalizing in many cases.

Guns

I've been immersed in occupations of service that require the use of guns my entire career, and guns have been given far more power and mystique in the public's mind than they deserve. We often find in mass shootings that dead bodies are piled against a wall or in a corner, the very place where the victims, frozen by fear, waited while the smaller and weaker active shooter paused and stepped out into the hallway to reload his weapons only to return and continue to kill. Why do people wait to be killed instead of fighting back? Because they have the false belief that the one with the gun has all the power. This is not true. You will learn in this book that the one with the gun has very little power, and that taking his gun away is usually a simple maneuver that every one of my schoolteacher trainees can easily perform.

We call the disarming maneuver The Inside Leverage Takeaway.

We don't discuss the politics of guns or public mental health in this book or in our training programs. These are important issues that demand our time and attention, but if you ever find yourself face to face with an active shooter, the only thing that matters in that moment is successfully defending yourself and others by eliminating that immediate threat. Our training takes into consideration the reality that an active shooter has entered a school or other facility with the intent to shoot innocent people. I know that approximately 99 percent of everyone present at a mass shooting is unarmed, and those are the people I train. We are committed to giving those people the tools they need to survive.

School Shooter

Most school shooters are playing a game—one in which they try to top the score (body count) of previous 'players.' They seek long-term fame after their death—which they assume will be within minutes of entering the school. Therefore, they are in a hurry to kill as many innocent, unprotected victims as possible in the shortest timeframe possible. When the score is run up and police close in, the school shooter is very likely to take his own life. Game over. Knowing this helps us formulate the best method to counter a school shooter and minimize the damage he causes during his rampage.

Workplace Shooter

Many workplace shootings are revenge attacks—often disgruntled or recently fired employees who have decided to kill his associates in the workplace. There will likely be specific targets, plus others who randomly get in his way. These often end in suicide, but some may seek to escape and stay alive. Knowing and understanding this helps us plan and respond appropriately. Many workplace shootings are domestic violence related—a boyfriend or husband who is determined to kill a specific woman who is employed at the company. He may be willing to shoot some others in the process, but his real target is the woman. He is likely to take his own life rather than be arrested and imprisoned. Understanding this reality helps us plan for and respond to many work-place shootings.

Terror Shooter

A domestic or foreign terrorist, is like the school shooter in that his goal is a high body count. Beyond body count, he seeks to create long-lasting mayhem and terror in the minds of innocent citizens, rendering them afraid to live their daily lives. To this end, he will inflict the greatest amount of violence, in the most vulnerable location possible, and will welcome the arrival of law enforcement officers, for which he will be prepared. He relishes the opportunity to exchange gunfire with police, to fight against the 'evil' government and convince the citizens that their government is helpless to defend them.

3 Minutes

When the nation was shocked by the cold-blooded attack on students within the walls of Columbine High School in Colorado, the harshest reality was that the killers who walked unimpeded through the school randomly shooting innocent, helpless students had plenty of time to do their evil work. Law enforcement, including patrol and SWAT Teams, were trained to approach the situation differently at that time. They would arrive quickly on the scene, and immediately commence rescue of injured students. As more units arrived, patrol officers would set up a perimeter and establish a command center. Officers would continue to rescue and treat anyone they could while the local SWAT Teams were deployed to the scene. SWAT would arrive with highly trained tactical specialists who would then methodically move through the building checking behind every door and in every room on their way to the shooter's location. By the time the SWAT Team members finally reached the Columbine shooters, they were long since dead from self-inflicted gunshot wounds. A total of 45 minutes had elapsed.

Since that time our law enforcement agencies have

retooled and retrained to face this new mass shooter phenomenon, and every officer and agent within a few miles of an active shooter situation is trained to speed to the location. In most jurisdictions, officers are trained to enter the premises immediately, waiting for no one, and to sprint to the source of the gunfire and immediately engage the shooter. They are running past injured citizens, through broken glass and smoke filled hallways, around blind corners and into the room where the shooter is located. They are running into the gunfight because every second counts. Every second they shave off their response time may be a life saved! In many jurisdictions the time between the first shot and an officer confronting the shooter is no more than 3 minutes. That is a herculean accomplishment of our law enforcement agencies around this great nation, and our communities should be filled with pride and gratitude for the brave men and women who have been trained and are willing to rush into the firefight to save lives.

Creating a plan to protect kids and survive for 3 to 5 minutes until the first officers arrive on the scene and engage the shooter is much more manageable than the extended time frames of the past. The evolution of our nation's law enforcement agencies in response to the active shooter problem is amazing and very effective. My mission is to help schools, corporations and the public evolve as well. My goal is to share training, information and techniques that enable them to be their own first responder until the police arrive.

Run – Hide – Fight

The designated program for most active shooter scenarios is to run away from the danger if possible, or to hide in a secure place, or to fight back as a last resort. I agree with this hierarchy of responses, and teach the specifics of each in our training courses. We keep it simple, so it will be effective.

Running and hiding are mostly intuitive natural survival reactions that have been taught and practiced for years. Fighting has not been intuitive or natural in active shooter situations, but that needs to change which is why most of our training and much of this book is dedicated to why, when and how to effectively fight back. Those who are harmed in mass shootings are usually those who were unable to run away or adequately hide and did not fight back. If confronted with an armed lunatic, most people simply give in to their fate, because they feel powerless to avoid the 'inevitable.' Of course, the reality is completely the opposite, and I dedicate my life to empowering teachers and others to fight back in a way that maximizes their survivability and minimizes the danger to them and those that they are trying to protect.

Run — If you can get away safely, do it! In our training we teach attendees to always have a primary and secondary escape route in mind. If the primary escape route is blocked you already have plan B. Your secondary (or alternate) route may not be as direct as your first choice—but it should lead you away from the trouble and eventually out of harm's way. Get far away from the trouble as quickly as possible, and call 9-1-1. Be sure to describe to the 9-1-1 operator:

1. The shooter and what he is wearing,
2. Any weapons and equipment he has,
3. His location and direction he was moving.

Hide — If you can't run – Hide! Hide so you can't be found, and if possible, barricade yourself so the shooter can't get to you, or is slowed too much to get to you in time, is the next best option. Remember you only need to buy yourself 3 to 5 minutes before law enforcement arrive on the scene. Many of those in an active shooter situation will be in this category. *Hide* means put yourself behind something so the shooter can't easily see you. Remember, he's looking for easy targets. If you can, get behind something that stops bullets, or stops the shooter from getting to you. We call this ***cover***. When you fortify your position to block his access we call it ***barricading***. Something that hides you but won't stop bullets is called **concealment**. Though it does not provide a physical bullet resistant barrier, sometimes just being able to stay out of sight of the shooter is enough to keep you alive. And as we've discussed, thanks to the training and heroism of local law enforcement agencies, in most cases you will only need to hide or barricade yourself for a few minutes before the police are on-site. Nearly all schools K—12, have locking classroom doors. Unfortunately, most college class-room doors often don't lock—so barricade!

Fight — If you can get away from an active shooter, get away. If the fight is brought to you, you ***must*** fight back. You can minimize the damage the shooter will do by fighting back. A number of school shooters have been stopped by people who fight back—even without this training. Fighting back works! If you fail to fight back, the shooter will inflict the maximum amount of damage unchecked until the first responders arrive and engage him in a gunfight. We discuss this in much greater detail later in this book, but for now, here's a brief description of what you do if you find yourself in an active shooter situation.

1. Get yourself and others into a room;
2. Turn off the lights in the room (it will take his eyes a few seconds to adjust as he comes from a brighter environment);
3. Lock the door if possible;
4. Barricade the door with any desks, sofas, tables or other furnishings in the room, then place a couple of your bodies on the floor, holding the barricades in place

like a human doorstop. This added resistance to the barricade can prevent the shooter from opening the door;

5. If the shooter does enter the room, aggressively counter attack him. This needs to be up close and person-al. No hitting or throwing items. Get inside arm's length. You can use The Inside Leverage Takeaway disarming technique to immediately disarm and subdue him until police arrive. (We have taught this effective disarming technique to thousands of teach-ers) Do whatever it takes to control him.

For demonstrations of these methods, see our 5-minute Active Shooter and The Inside Leverage Takeaway video at FightBackNation.org/video. Note: the woman who performs the Takeaway in the Active Shooter video learned it in a practice session one hour before the video was shot.

There it is. I know it seems simple, but in most cases, these simple things are not being done, and victims are being needlessly killed in mass shootings.

Now it's time to roll up our sleeves and get to work. I'll explain these concepts and techniques in greater detail now, and help you understand the WHY? and HOW behind everything, to give you the confidence you need to face the unthinkable if it ever happens to you.

Let's start with the evolution of Law Enforcement.

Chapter One —3 Minutes

Officer 1, call sign Charlie 3, ran toward the school with his AR-15 held tight against his chest, stopping to peer around the corner of a concrete pillar to see if the shooter could be seen inside the school from this location. Nothing yet. Alarms were blaring and he tried to control his heavy breaths for a second as he strained to hear the gunshots ringing from inside. He glanced back and saw Officer 2, call sign Charlie 9, running at top speed toward his position. He looked back at the building and through the glass windows where he could see the reception desk. It was empty, but he caught a brief glimpse of blond hair moving away from the desk. Pop, pop, pop! Shots rang out from somewhere inside, and he decided not to wait the 15 seconds before Charlie 9 reached his position. Every second counted. Every shot could be an innocent student being murdered. He had to get to the shooter immediately. One minute or less at this point. He sprinted for the front doors, and crouched below the glass windows, struggling to peek over the top where he could get a better look inside. There was no movement. Charlie 9 crouched beside him and asked, "See anything?"

"Nothing."

He looked again and could see nothing, just as three more shots rang out inside somewhere making him jump. He hesitated, then gathered his courage, and peeked through the window again. "I say we go in."

"Can you see the shooter?" Charlie 9 asked.

"I can't see anything. They said get to the shooter ASAP, so we gotta move out."

The officers reluctantly stood in a bending position and cautiously pushed their way through the doors and into the front office reception area. Alarms were ringing loudly. They quickly scurried through the office and saw two women crouched behind desks in the back.

"Do you know where the shooter is?" Charlie 3 asked them. They shook their heads in unison, unable to speak. "Okay—clear this area. Evacuate!" He pointed toward the front door and the women instinctively put their hands on their heads and rushed outside through the glass doors.

The officers saw steel-framed double doors leading to the main hallway of the school. The doors were closed, blocking them from proceeding further down the hall. To the side of the closed double doors were 18-inch-wide glass panels laced with wire (still found in older schools). It was through these glass panels that they saw a student bleeding from the chest holding tight to another student with a massive head wound lying still next to a large puddle of blood. They looked at each other briefly then ran forward to get through the door. They crashed against the double doors, with little effect other than a loud thud. The door did not budge.

"What the f*&@"! Charlie 9 groaned as he bounced back on his toes. The officers tried the door again, only to find it was locked, and the bar to open it was on the other side.

Charlie 3 cued his mic and asked dispatch, "Why are the interior doors locked?"

"Are the alarms sounding"? someone asked over the radio.

"Yeah."

"There's an auto lock system on fire doors when the alarms are pulled. You can only exit when the system is engaged. You can't enter deeper into the building."

"Damn!" Charlie 9 said, pushing violently against the doors. They didn't budge. He kicked the middle of the doors hoping to dislodge the magnetic lock holding the doors closed. Same result; nothing. Under immense stress the officers failed to realize that the doors would only open in one direction; out toward the officers.

Charlie 3 banged hard on the glass panel and got the attention of the boy lying about eight feet on the other side of the door with a chest wound and what he could now see was a bullet hole in his thigh. He banged hard again, then pointed to the opening bar on the other side of the door and shouted, "Open the door so we can get through!" The wounded student shook his head as he cried, and indicated that he couldn't get to the door to open it. Charlie 3 banged the doors harder and shouted, "Open this door! We gotta get in and stop the shooter!"

The wounded student almost seemed to ignore the officers now, and turned toward his dead friend and screamed through his tears putting his hand over the bleeding wound on his own chest.

Charlie 9 continued to pound on the metal part of the door, causing even Charlie 3 to jump. The wounded student just ignored them, doing his best to wake the student lying dead near him.

The officers continued to pound on the door and shouted instructions to the wounded student, to no avail. After two more minutes of this they finally saw another officer enter from a side door, which they hadn't noticed before. He ran to their door and pushed the bar, opening the doors for them. He then turned and ran down a hallway to the right, while Charlie 3 and Charlie 9 hurried straight ahead into the hallway before them. They heard more gunfire ringing out ahead of them. About sixty feet later they arrived at a T-intersection of the hall and turned right where they encountered two more students down on the floor with multiple gunshot wounds. Their new instructions were to move past the wounded and get to the shooter immediately and stop him from shooting anyone else. They had already lost too much time stuck at the front hallway door, and hurried past the corner to where the wounded students lay bleeding.

"Don't worry," Charlie 3 comforted as he passed them, "help is right behind us."

He continued past the two wounded students, and was surprised as he tripped and nearly fell as someone grabbed his foot. He regained his balance and looked over to see that one of the wounded was holding his boot.

"Let go!" he commanded, but the grip didn't loosen at all.

"My brother's dying! Help him!"

Charlie 3 looked at Charlie 9, who shot him a quick shake of the head. Charlie 3 tried to pull away so he could rush toward the new shots that filled the hallway somewhere ahead, but the wounded student wouldn't let him go.

"Let go, kid," Charlie 3 insisted, trying to free himself.

"You gotta help him. He's been shot! He needs help! You can't let him die!"

While Charlie 3 attempted to free himself Charlie 9 finally decided that he should move forward, continuing down the hallway as Charlie 3 argued with the poor wounded student. Within seconds Charlie 3 was with him again and they turned another corner to find smoke obscuring their ability to see down the hallway.

"What the f#@*," Charlie 9 said, "Did they set the place on fire?"

Just then two flashes of muzzle fire streaked through the smoky hallway and the two officers returned fire, shooting several shots into the smoke in the direction of the bright flashes.

Charlie 3 took a second to cue his mic and said, "We've engaged the shooter in the south hallway," but just as he said it they heard shots pounding the air in a distant room. Confused, they took cover as more muzzle fire flashed in the hallway through the smoke, and they returned fire again. They waited a minute to see if the shooter would fire back, but they heard nothing in the smoke before them, so they decided to rush the shooter if he was still there. They held their AR-15s tightly in front of them and ran through the smoke and screaming alarms until they reached another turn in the hallway. There was very little smoke ahead so they ran at full speed toward the sound of screams and shots being fired in classrooms just 30 feet ahead. Their hearts pounded as they approached the door and two people suddenly burst out of the room, almost colliding with the officers. Instinctively they fired their weapons, shooting the threats, then watching them fall to the ground in horror as they realized they were students escaping the shots fired inside the room.

The officers were sickened and panicked as they realized what they had done, but jumped through the doorway and instantly scanned through the smoke for the shooter. In front of them was a man lying prostrate screaming, "Don't shoot. I give up!"

More shots rang out in the room next door, and the officers were completely confused. Now it appeared that two shooters had committed this mayhem, and now one of them was surrendering. They weren't sure what to do, because there was no way that just one of them should take on the remaining shooter alone—their best hope of getting him was trapping him in crossfire. A one-on-one gunfight made things much more difficult. Feeling they had no choice, Charlie 9 dropped down and put his knee in the surrendering shooter's back as he reached for his handcuffs. Charlie 3 hurried back out through the door and ran to the next room where he heard gunfire and crouched down to create a lower profile as he scanned for the shooter inside. The shooter jumped behind a desk and continued to fire his weapon, smoke rolling freely from the rifle's hot barrel. Charlie 3 felt the hand of another officer at his back and together they stormed the room, Charlie 3 going right and the other officer going left, catching the shooter in their crossfire, finally ending the rampage.

* * *

The mayor, who was inside the school observing the training scenario, was nearly in tears as he doubled over ready to vomit. "If anyone ever attacks our schools, we're going to fail these kids." He was visibly shaken, vacillating between anger and despair.

I put my arm around his shoulder and said, "Mayor—just wait until the end of the day. You'll see. Give us 'til the end of the day."

Yes—it was a school shooter simulation drill, conducted by my team for the police department of a small Western town. After the Columbine school shooting massacre, our non-profit, the National Foundation for Officer Survival Training (NFOST) was contracted to provide active shooter training for local law enforcement at the town high school. The high school drama teacher set up moulage makeup stations and dozens of students looked like they were suffering from severe injuries, transforming this into one of the best scenario-based trainings I've ever been involved in. Because it was a small town I expected a handful of police officers to be involved, but there were 18 of them present, along with a couple of dedicated dispatchers running the communications radio systems, and recording the entire event.

I spoke with the students beforehand and explained that in a live mass shooter scenario, victims and friends and relatives of victims would be desperate to get the officers to stop and help the wounded—so to do everything in their power to get the officers to divert their attention from the active shooter. "If your brother or sister was shot and dying, you would grab the first cop that came through and say, 'Please help my brother. He's been shot and I think he's dying,' and you wouldn't let go of him until he helped your brother. So do that." I added, "If you were injured and bleeding to death, and you saw a cop walk by you would do everything you could to get him to stop and help you, so you wouldn't die. You would scream, 'Help me! Help me!' and you wouldn't let him go." They didn't quite understand why I gave them these instructions, but they followed my directions—and the results were devastating for the officers who were being subjected to their cries for help for the first time.

Before Columbine, the first SWAT Team members (a two-member "cell") on the scene would step past the victims, and let the cell behind them grab the wounded and drag them back to safety—waiting for them to return before proceeding. Then the same would happen when they would come upon the next wounded, and so on. This was a widely accepted and practiced citizen rescue technique. They would also check behind every door, and clear every room, to ensure that there were no bad guys that could escape or double back and attack from behind. It was a slow and deliberate process that prioritized security over speed, and served law enforcement teams well for decades. It greatly slowed the process of stopping the carnage. Keep in mind, to this point we had rarely encountered active shooters conducting a mass shooting with such a well thought out and long lasting engagement. Now, after a major retraining program throughout the nation, the protocol is for every officer arriving on the scene to speed past the wounded and the open doors toward the gunfire and engage the shooter immediately. We teach them that they are the hunter, and their number one job is to quickly track down the shooter and stop him—put him down! "Ice in your veins," we teach them. "You go directly to the gunfire and stop the shooter." **Then,** after the shooter is neutralized or taken into custody, they are able to begin rescuing the wounded.

This was a difficult transition for police officers like me who had been trained to clear rooms methodically unless it was a hostage rescue, wherein we would take the quickest route to the X (point of engagement) and execute the rescue. Now the new active shooter response protocol was essentially a large-scale movement at hostage rescue speed. And it makes sense. Essentially this is a more urgent hostage rescue. Every second counts. Every passing second could mean a life lost. Every second saved by economy of movement and decisive action could mean a life saved. New officers are trained to do it this way in the police academy, so it is completely natural to them. They come out of the academy competent and confident and will sprint toward an active shooter to stop him.

In the first run of this active shooter drill staged at the local high school, everything had gone wrong. The first two officers on the scene:

1. Got bogged down at the first hall fire doors, unable to influence the "wounded student" on the other side to open the doors to let them pass. They got into a shouting match with him. Their brains quickly shut down so they didn't notice the simple solution to their access problem-another door just a few feet and few seconds away. They had quickly descended into what we call "Condition Black."

2. The next thing they did was get stopped by students with wounded friends and relatives.

3. The adversary they engaged in the smoky hallway turned out to be a flashing strobe light set 12 feet above the floor to guide students through smoke filled corridors during fires. They later learned that the smoke came from the shooters' shells as they fired (blanks produce the same amount of smoke as live rounds), and had set off the fire alarms, which had automatically locked the hallway fire doors.

4. The officers who had just gone through the drill complained that their radios weren't working correctly—that there was no communication from dispatch following the incident with the hall doors. The two dispatchers who were working the drill played their recordings for everyone involved, and the officers discovered that the radios were working perfectly the entire time—but they suffered personal audio shutdown due to stress; their ears failed to hear radio broadcasts during the action.

The responding officers had gone into what we call Condition Black—suffering from extreme tunnel vision and auditory shutdown. This is a natural physiological response to high level stress. The one-minute hunt for the shooters had become nine minutes, and hundreds of rounds were fired while the officers ambled, confused and mentally overloaded toward the gunfire. The mayor was beside himself, upset at the horrible performance of his police force. Nonetheless, we ran the drill three or four more times with different sets of officers, to see how they fared. We did not allow the previous groups of officers to discuss their experience with the following teams, as we wanted each group to work through at least one scenario without previous knowledge of what was coming. It was essentially the same with each run-through. The high school kids and staff reset each time, pouring out more fake blood, getting into position, all ready to act like they likely would in the event of a real rampage through their school. Each set of officers suffered similar troubles.

I consoled the mayor and police chief, assuring them that by the end of our training, they and the teachers and staff would know exactly what to do. These amazing cops did not let me down. They were resilient and hungry to improve. They were determined and committed. By the end of the day, the police force acted like a well-oiled machine. Not surprisingly to me, the role-players we asked to be the shooters—also police officers—found it nearly impossible to do any damage in subsequent drills. Success. I will never forget an emotional and tearful Mayor as he praised these brave police officers. He was candid in his comments as he related to them his first impressions. He apologized for ever doubting them. He, like the rest of us, can rest easy at night, knowing that these incredible men and women will be there charging in to face these evil cowards and they will put them down without hesitation.

As the officers run through repeated training scenarios, they get used to the distractions, and they are able to focus on what's truly important, using all of their best instincts to locate and stop the shooter. The lesson I emphasize during their training:

"The chaos manages you, or you manage it."

The lesson was learned, and the responding officers managed the chaos and moved through the school confidently, even though in subsequent drills the shooters changed the scenarios. After a few training runs, the shooters lasted less than 60 seconds. This is one small example, a peek into a tiny sliver of the remarkable evolution our amazing law enforcement professionals have gone through on their way to a 3 minute response time.

Chapter Two — Warrior DNA

Extraordinary people do extraordinary things. What most people don't realize is that ordinary people also do extraordinary things. I developed a theory about what I have come to call the Warrior Switch, which resides within most of us, and can be flipped "ON" to ensure survival in extraordinary circumstances. In an effort to share this theory I created a non-profit law enforcement training entity named the " National Foundation for Officer Survival Training" or NFOST for short.

When I was in the police academy we received training intended to prepare us for life threatening circumstances, and to help us keep a clear head so we could use the skills they taught us to avoid harm or worse. The technology we enjoy today was not available then, but they did have recordings of patrol radio traffic during several harrowing situations we could listen to, visualizing the circumstances of the officers involved. In one of those recordings we heard the pleas for help of a police officer who was shot and pinned down behind his patrol car. The suspect had a high-powered rifle and kept all would be rescuers away from him. Over a period of ten minutes we heard the life drain out of the desperate officer as he pleaded for his fellow-officers to come to his aid and save his life. We were told that the officer died before the others could get to him. What was truly tragic about the death of the young officer was that when the others located him, they found that his wound was to his arm, and that he had failed to apply a tourniquet to stop the bleeding. That simple act of first aid would likely have saved his life. He chose to rely on others to rescue him.

The point we learned was that at one far end of the spectrum there are people who are faced with life-threatening circumstances, who simply accept their fate and do almost nothing to preserve their lives. At the other end of the spectrum were critically wounded officers who found a way to survive, regardless of the obstacles. I thought about that a lot, and wondered what the difference might be.

Enrique Hernandez

As we were teaching safety and survival techniques to police officers around the nation, certain cases began to come to my attention, illustrating the point that when the stakes become quite high, people step up and do whatever it takes to survive perilous situations. Enrique Hernandez was a young police officer in the Las Vegas Metro Police Department, and had recently been assigned to his own patrol car. He got into a vehicle pursuit with a suspect, who during the chase ended up crashing his car. He jumped out of the damaged vehicle and fled on foot. Enrique pursued him calling out over his radio, "Edward 35, foot pursuit, foot pursuit". He followed the suspect into an apartment building and through an open door. His radio went silent, for just 12 seconds, then he cued his mic and spoke rapidly, "444, Officer Down! I've been shot. I'm bleeding bad! Multiple wounds!"

My expertise is in tactical procedures, providing law enforcement and special tactical units with the training and tools they need to survive close threats, like armed suspects in enclosed environments. Enrique's experience is a 'worst case scenario' I wanted to understand better. Enrique found himself in an overwhelming circumstance, and as he moved through the apartment he saw there was a sliding glass door leading out the back of the kitchen. He aimed his gun carefully at the open door in case the suspect was still lurking just outside the door waiting for him. As he entered the kitchen with his attention on the sliding glass door, he caught a glimpse of a gun barrel directly to his right. Instantly he swung around, trying to get his own gun on target before the suspect fired. The barrel exploded and a .357 magnum bullet fired through his left forearm, the impact of the bullet, knocking his left hand off of his gun. He immediately tried to bring his injured hand back to his firearm. Before he could re-grip his gun, the next round went through his left hand and impacted his neck. The tiny kitchen exploded in a deafening volley of gunfire, Enrique and the suspect exchanging bullets only three feet apart from each other. Enrique's round went through the suspect's armpit and exited his back. However, at the same time a third shot struck Enrique in the chest, where it lodged in his bullet proof vest. The shots rang out in rapid succession, the next one shattering the bones in Enrique's right arm. In mere seconds he had been shot in his left forearm, through his left hand, his neck, his chest and now his right forearm, disabling his gun hand. It was at this point Enrique realized he was unable to return fire and turned to escape the kitchen. As he turned to exit the kitchen, the suspect fired two more rounds.

Unfortunately for Enrique, one of those bullets found the small gap between the side panels in his body armor and hit him in the ribs, deflecting around to his vertebrae. The last round went through his leg as he exited the kitchen.

Enrique made it to the front yard and collapsed, struggling for breath. His body was already hoarding blood in his core, starving his extremities. He was fast losing feeling in his hands and arms, but he was able to cue his mic and tell dispatch he was down in the front yard. With his last burst of strength Enrique drew his knife and planned to defend his life with his knife if the shooter came back to finish him off. "If I'm gonna die, you're gonna die," was the thought that kept him conscious until help arrived. A short time later the suspect was found and killed during a confrontation with the SWAT team. Enrique survived.

Survival Instinct

I learned an important lesson from Enrique Hernandez. Humans have a survival instinct. Yeah, I knew that before. But as I heard Enrique recount his experience, and as I lived it and relived it with him listening to the radio recording, I began to understand just how profound that instinct is—and how there seems to be a switch that we can throw "ON" when we are triggered by a serious event or threat. I immediately thought of the momma bear instinct that many mothers have reported, and the concept of flipping the survival switch began to take shape in my mind. It was a watershed moment in my evolving understanding of human survival.

Our NFOST training on officer survival began to emphasize the "survivor mentality," and the ability to flip that "ON" when needed. Our training merged physical fitness with mental toughness and a few basic skills to transform police officers into unstoppable forces, when lives depended on it.

We arrived in Phoenix, Arizona to provide an officer survival training session, and during a short break that day were asked if we would be willing to present our training to 10 people in a special session. Some of those in the session were battle-tested warriors, one having been severely wounded.

"Have you ever been in a shooting?" he asked.

"Yes."

"Have you ever been shot?"

"Yeah."

"Okay."

That was the toughest interview I had ever been through, and I only spoke two words. *Tough crowd*. Literally.

He took a seat with the others and I began my presentation. I watched him and the other nine during the seminar and they all responded visibly as I shared the story of Enrique Hernandez, conveying my gut feeling that there is an internal strength we can switch "ON" that helps us overcome any level of adversity, as long as we remain willing. After the presentation I asked some of the other attendees about the story behind the young man with the cane. They related that one night a few months before, he was shot numerous times while trying to make an arrest. He ended up in a fight with the suspect and had him on the ground, but because it was so dark he was unable to see the suspect pull out a gun from his waist band. The suspect fired several shots, and all of the bullets traveled upward under the officer's body armor into his abdomen. Back-up was struggling to locate the critically wounded officer in the dark. Somehow, he managed to remain conscious and climb a fence where he could better guide responding officers to his location. He coded on the way to the hospital and the medical teams had to work on him extensively to keep him alive. He became a supporter of NFOST and his experience was added to our roster of those who had found the will to persevere after others would have succumbed.

Later that day during the other presentations to the Phoenix group, other officers came forward with similar experiences, perhaps even more harrowing, buttressing my point that there is a switch inside most of us, which we are able to flip "ON" if we perceive a great enough threat. It occurred to me that I should invite these heroes to the microphone to share their stories, and as I listened my feelings were confirmed as I witnessed a pattern begin to emerge. Over the next several trainings I actively sought out similar survivors in the groups and invited them to share their experiences from the front of the room.

My theory about this type of person (or trait) really began to gel in my mind. There was a type of person who was a survivor, and when threatened with death—their own, or that of an innocent person they cared about—their switch was flipped and they found the strength to survive and overcome. It occurred to me that we were presenting our courses to a certain type of person—one who had already made the decision to pursue a career to "Protect and Serve" people they didn't know personally. Perhaps, I wondered, this survive and protect "switch" was more prevalent in this type of person. I learned about a book titled *On Killing: The Psychological Cost of Learning to Kill in War and Society*, by Lt. Col. Dave Grossman, wherein he expresses his belief that people with the protective proclivity tend to find their way into military and public safety careers, including police, firefighters, first responders, medical personnel, etc.

My life was centered in teaching police officers to survive in harrowing circumstances. I gave a lot of thought to the matter of those who are better able to step up in desperate circumstances, to preserve themselves, or others. I had begun to read about experiences where everyday people would often step up and show extraordinary valor for themselves or for perfect strangers. It occurred to me that the ON SWITCH seems to exist in most people. The only question is, what does it take to flip it to the "ON" position? Across the spectrum of people and the careers they chose I found that there is a survival instinct that appears to be built right into our DNA—what I often refer to as our Warrior DNA.

As I began to speak about this SWITCH, I found that I was getting a little resistance from some of the attendees at our seminars. Some would come up to me and say, "Hey, I'm not that guy." They would relate how they just didn't have those feelings of rushing headlong into the face of danger, or worse, and saving the day. For them, hanging back and letting "the specialists" handle the crisis was the answer. "I'm not going in there." "That's a job for the SWAT team." "I didn't get hired to commit suicide."

The Momma Bear Trigger

I was addressing a group of 200 citizens one day, and one of them spoke up and candidly admitted in front of all of the others that he just did not see himself as a hero. Keep in mind this is a big guy, about six feet tall and built like a linebacker. Notwithstanding his size and obvious fitness, he said, "Dave, I'm a gun guy. I know what an AR-15 can do. If an AR is pointed in my direction, all I'm gonna accomplish is think of all of the stuff I've done wrong in my life, because I'm about to meet Jesus."

I looked at him for a minute, wondering why someone so capable was saying he could not and would not act when his life depended on decisive action. He was telling the entire group that he lacked the Warrior DNA. How could it be?

"It just doesn't make sense to me that I could fight through that," he added.

"Okay," I said, sizing him up. He looked about 50 to me, and because he lived in a state where having families early in life is normal, I asked if he had any grandchildren.

"Yeah," he said, looking at me with a question in his eyes. I have a grandson. He's six."

I have a few little grandchildren as well, and I know how I feel about them. So I assumed I could help him find his inner Warrior if we could trigger his inner Momma Bear. I had the orange plastic training AR-15 in my hands to demonstrate the disarming technique we teach. I said to him, "Okay, your six year old grandson is right there," pointing the rifle about six feet from him, "and I point this AR at him. What are you gonna do?"

His eyes grew twice their normal size and he stood up and pointed his finger at me and was almost enraged as he said, "That's not funny! Don't even think about that!"

I could see that something had clicked inside him, and that his Warrior Switch was in the "ON" position. "What's wrong?" I asked him. "Why are you upset? What are you going to do about it? What would you do right now?"

"I'd be on top of you so fast. I'd rip your head off!" He was suddenly very aggressive—very protective.

"Thank you," I said, and all 200 people in the auditorium began clapping. There it was. The Momma Bear Trigger had switched his Warrior DNA to "ON."

Here's the principle:

We don't always hold our own life in the
same high regard as we hold that of a loved one.

This grandfather would run through gunfire and strangle the life out of me if his grandson were in danger—the same person who just couldn't see himself grabbing the weapon away from me if his own life were on the line. So much can change in a few seconds.

So these questions arise: "How would your children and grandchildren feel if anything happened to you? Would it hurt them? Would they grieve? Would it disrupt their lives? Would it affect them?"

The answer is an obvious yes, and I allow that to sink in, inviting my trainees to really contemplate the cost of their own loss. After they've had a chance to think it through, most of them come to understand that protecting their own life is nearly as important as protecting the lives of their loved ones—and for very similar reasons.

Momma Bear x 10

Let's go to the next category of Momma Bear. Teachers. I have people on my team who are international experts on mass shootings. When I first suggested that Fight Back Nation begin to go into schools and train teachers to fight back against mass shooters, they said things like, "Dave— these are teachers. They are usually female. They are patient, and loving, and sweet, and kind, and empathetic, etc. They aren't like law enforcement officers. It's not in their nature to physically engage and fight back."

My response: "Really? So you're telling me that these are loving, protective, empathetic people who devote their lives to loving other peoples children all day every day—30 strangers' children in every class. Who has a greater capacity to love children more than a teacher? What kind of a person says to others, bring me your children and let me provide education, understanding and compassion all day? Believe me—teachers have a tremendous capacity to love these children, and they devote their lives to them. Let those children be put into mortal danger, and you will see Momma Bear syndrome on steroids." In fact, most teachers have giant hearts, even though the children don't always see it. Their capacity to love is multiplied. Their Momma Bear reaction to a threat is also multiplied. I have seen it thousands of times since that first discussion. Many teachers have simply put their bodies in front of the children in their classes during mass shootings. It's sad, because there are safer, more productive things they can do to protect the children—but their willingness to protect their students with their own lives is the most admirable of all human qualities. "No one has greater love than this: to lay down his life for his friends." (John 15:13)

All Juab School District employees are Fight Back Nation trained and certified. Juab is the first Fight Back Nation certified School District in the US. Nephi Utah.

The truth is that many people feel so small and helpless that they've spent their lives believing they are powerless if confronted by force. Many accept that they would simply give up and give in, accepting whatever fate an aggressor had determined for them.

Fighting back to protect the innocent is the great equalizer. Almost everyone's Warrior DNA is ignited when an innocent victim is threatened with imminent harm. Personal fear and incredible odds take a backseat to the sudden necessity of stepping into the breach and doing everything humanly possible to protect the innocent one.

ANSWER: We give teachers and others a technique to protect children that is simple,

practical and effective. A technique that gives
them a much better chance to survive.

We support teachers' Momma Bear instinct, and provide
them with the tools to go Momma Bear Extraordinaire –
Momma Bear times 10.

Size doesn't matter. A small female teacher uses the
information and technique to disarm a mass shooter as he
tries to enter the classroom. That's the training we give
them. Every teacher learns it. Every teacher executes it
successfully.

Now, when a small female teacher says to me, "Dave, in
that extreme moment when it comes down to it, and you're
asking me to wait around a corner for a crazed man twice my
size to come through the door with an AR-15, intent on
killing me and all of my students, you expect me to find the
inner strength to attack him and take his rifle from him?"

"Yes, I do."

She has trouble processing that, until the very moment
when it dawns on her, to her very core, that her inaction will
allow the deaths of those children. I give her the example of
the child falling in a rushing river, and she realizes that there
is something inside of her that simply will not allow a child
to die like that. She would jump in without hesitation
regardless of the risk to her. Now she makes the connection,
in that moment size no longer matters, and strength no
longer matters. The weapon doesn't even matter. Nothing
matters except the reality that as long as she's fighting that
man, he's not shooting her children. At that moment she
opens to the realization that I'm giving her a tool to keep
those children alive. The better she pays attention and learns
The Inside Leverage Takeaway disarming technique, the
better her chances are of surviving and saving those
children. It's really that simple.

Chapter Three — Let's Get Our Terms Straight

Let's talk about some concepts and definitions. The more you know about the weapons, equipment, methods and mindset of the psychos that shoot innocent people, the better your chances of surviving an attack.

Firearms

As we discussed in the beginning, guns have a cultural mystique, and those who wield them are often believed to possess all power over those who don't have them. Indeed, most mass shooters feel that they are in "God Mode" during their attack—which is a computer game reference wherein your avatar cannot be harmed or killed by his opponents for a period of time. By discussing the true nature of guns, we strip them of their mystique, and help you understand that they are simply a hand-held mechanical device; with limitations and vulnerabilities.

There are two basic gun types used in active and mass shootings.

1. The semi-automatic pistol; or
2. The semi-automatic rifle.

What are the important facts to know about these two types of weapons?

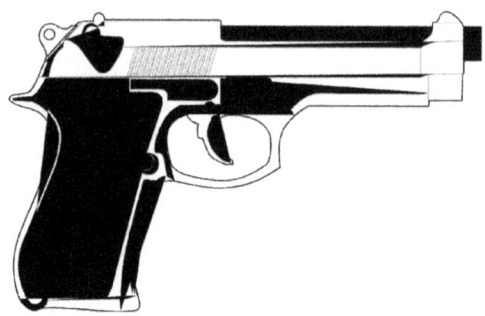

#1 — The semi-automatic pistol is most accurate inside of 30 or 40 feet. It's difficult to hit a moving target. It's used for self-protection. The shooter squeezes the trigger to fire a shot, and can shoot them in rapid succession. After 12 to 15 shots, he's out of bullets. Reloading is relatively simple.

#2 — The semi-automatic AR or AK style rifle will generally have larger magazine capacity options—often 30 rounds. Rifles shoot accurately for much longer distances than pistols, accurate well beyond 100 feet. Their bullets may be able to penetrate some body armor. Regardless of their general accuracy, it is still hard to hit a moving target.

*If you are reporting a shooting on a 9-1-1
call, it is important for responding officers to
know the type of weapon(s) being used—to help
them determine the type of weapon they should
grab as they rush in to save lives.*

Now that you understand the types of weapons shooters are using, it will help you better realize that they can usually only squeeze off one shot at a time, and that they are not actually in *God Mode* during their rampage. Shooters can be disarmed and subdued in mere seconds, stopping the bloodshed immediately. More on that in chapter 10.

Types of Shootings

For the purposes of our discussion and the training we offer at Fight Back Nation, we are talking about two basic types of public shootings:

Active Shooter:
- Someone with ability (firearm)
- Intent/Action (shooting)
- Mobile

Mass Shooter:
- Single incident
- Single public location (except Midland TX shooting)
- At least 4 people or more shot

These definitions can overlap, but are not always inter-changeable. The differences are important, especially to law enforcement officers who need to stop the shooting—because they need to understand the motives and capabilities of the shooter. An active shooter is simply someone with the ability and intent to shoot someone, and who is actively mobile in that regard. A mass shooter is someone who shoots four or more people at a single public location. We say public location because we don't consider a gang shootout to be targeting innocent people in a location where there is an expectation of safety.

Shooter Classifications

School Shooters
- Numbers is the goal (body count)
- Can be multiple shooters

Terrorism
- Numbers is the goal (body count)
- Message to the World
- Can be multiple shooters

Personal
- Domestic or Revenge

An active shooter is a person who has the ability and has demonstrated that he intends to shoot someone. Perhaps his target is a specific person, or perhaps a group of people—he may or may not know the victims. He may have already fired a shot, or still intends to shoot. This means once he has started shooting, in an attempt to stay on the move, he can carjack a car and drive to a different location with his pistol in the seat next to him, and he is still an active shooter. Until the situation is brought to a conclusion, he is an active shooter. A mass shooter is someone who has shot 4 or more people at a single location. There have been some mass shooters who have shot 4 or more people at one location, then gone to a second location to shoot 4 or more people. These are two mass shooter sites. A mass shooter is an active shooter, and does not become a mass shooter until he shoots his fourth victim.

Targets
- Malls—Stores—Shopping
- Public Buildings
- Schools
- Businesses
- Hospitals
- Concerts—Theaters
- Open Public Areas

The motivations of active shooters, who never become mass shooters, are usually much different than those of the mass shooter. It is important to understand the different classifications of active shooters, though the fundamentals of disarming them remain the same.

Workplace Shooters
The #1 killer of men in the workplace is motor vehicle accidents. The #2 killer of men in the workplace is an accident/slip or fall. The #3 killer of men in the workplace accidentally being struck by an object.

In contrast, the #1 killer of women in the workplace is murder. This usually means that an ex husband or boyfriend comes to her workplace with the intent of killing her.

The workplace culture should be one that helps women feel safe enough to share any domestic violence issues they may be experiencing with their closest colleagues. At Fight Back Nation we have a hands-on seminar for women's empowerment and protection that we call the **Women's Empowerment and Personal Defense Seminar.**

If "Sally" informs her supervisor or workplace about a possible problem (threats of violence) from her ex, "Joe," and describes him and his vehicle, her fellow workers will be on the alert if they ever see Joe's truck pull up out front. They can go into immediate lockdown and call 9-1-1 to get law enforcement help there within mere minutes.

If Joe gets out of the truck and has trouble getting through the front glass doors, he might shoot them. If his intent was in doubt before, it's clear now—he's an Active Shooter. When talking to the police, let them know the facts that tell you that Joe is an Active Shooter, even if he hasn't shot anyone yet. That helps them to know what to look for and how to prepare when they arrive.

RUN—HIDE—FIGHT Steps

Run means **escape.** As we've discussed, your first choice in an active shooter or mass shooter event is to escape. To do this, wherever you are, always be aware of your surroundings, and notice the exits. In a place where you work or study, have a primary escape route, plus a secondary escape route. If you encounter trouble in your primary route, switch to your secondary route. I demonstrate this in our 5-minute Active Shooter video and The Inside Leverage Takeaway disarming technique video at FightBackNation.org/video.

Hide means conceal or cover.

Concealment means get behind something so the shooter can't see you.

Cover means get behind something that will stop a bullet.

Barricade means get behind something that makes it hard for him to get to you—fortify your hiding place.

Concealment
- Hiding Place
- Regular door
- Curtains
- Desks (behind not under)

Cover (provides protection from bullets)
- Thick wood door
- Steel
- Concrete wall
- Thick materials

Barricade
- Lock the door
- Turn off the lights
- Place desks, sofas, filing cabinets and other heavy items against the door
- Place yourselves at the base of those items so they can't be easily moved—at the base (on the floor) so shots fired through the door won't hit you
- Remain silent, and don't open the door

While you're running or hiding, law enforcement is sprinting as fast as they possibly can to the location of the shots to engage the shooter and stop the shooting. As a number of officers and agents race from their location at the time the call goes out to the site of the shooter, they are trying to collect as much information as they can to properly engage and stop the shooter. Following is the list of priorities in the training received by officers and agents.

Law Enforcement Response

First team goes directly to active shooter

- Terminate threats

Require Accurate direction and description

- Where is the shooter?
- How many shooters?
- What is shooter wearing?
- What is the shooter using as a weapon(s)?
- Does he have a duffle bag or backpack?
- What significant rooms are in the direction of the shooter?
- Where are the exits the shooter may use to escape?
- Shooter terminated
- Immediate rescue of injured
- Methodical clearing of school
- Clear parking areas and gathering areas of secondary devices
- Conduct interviews
- Release victims and witnesses

It is important for law enforcement to assess the threat as accurately as possible.

Important: Don't call 9-1-1 and guess about the type of weapon the shooter is using. If you call an AR-15 a shotgun, or vice versa, the responding officers may grab the wrong weapon when they rush into the gunfight with the shooter.

My own daughter is a young policewoman, and she is fully trained to rush into an active shooter situation and engage the shooter in a gun battle. I don't want her to have the wrong equipment when she risks her life for others. If the shooter has a rifle, I want her to know that, and be prepared for it. Rifles usually have a larger magazine that holds many more bullets—often up to 30. The bullets go faster and father, with more accuracy—and may penetrate police body armor. So if you see an active shooter with a rifle of some kind, be accurate in describing it to the dispatcher on the phone. If the shooter has a handgun, do your best to describe it.

Unfortunately, we are accumulating a database of active shooter and mass shooter details, and below are some highlights of the statistics that are beginning to take form.

Analysis of 93 Active Shooter Incidents
- 90% act alone
- 85% have rifles
- 75% have multiple weapons and hundreds of bullets
- Average target hit rate of 50%

Weapons Used
- Hand guns with multiple magazines
- Semi-auto rifles (often AR or AK style)
- Pipe bombs
- Knives (although they haven't used them often)

Training
- Pre-plan attacks

- Target practice
- Research of weapons and explosives

Mobility
- Ability to move from room to room
- Control hallways
- High volume locations (cafeteria or auditorium)
- Run from building to building
- Choose a location for last stand

In response to an active shooter or mass shooter, many government agencies have put together plans of how to deal with such an event. You may have received training in your employment that covers many of these same strategies.

Emergency Response Plan
- Lock Down Procedures
- Audio Alarm (different than fire alarm)
- Monitoring System (CCTV)
  - o Monitors in secure locations so law enforcement get real time updates
- Card system (red and green)
- Hall Clearing consolidating students without allowing shooter entry to your safe haven

Chapter Four — Welcome to Condition RED

There is a moment where our mind is perfectly tranquil, and entirely unaware of our surroundings. It is the most at peace and unaware during sleep. At the opposite end of the awareness spectrum is panic and inability to think or act. We operate in the middle most of the day, depending on our environment and assessment of the dangers around us.

Recognize, Assess and React

Because there are various levels of awareness and responsiveness to the things that happen in our lives, we should be conscious of them, and make sure they work for us, and not against us. Ideally, we should live in a state where we are consciously *recognizing* unusual people or conditions, *assessing* them for danger, and *reacting* appropriately to them. In the police academy and in SWAT training we have a color chart that helps us understand that there is an escalation of awareness levels that we naturally assume, based on our environment. The goal of this chapter is to help you get to that place in your own mind—to plant a seed that grows into an alert mindset, so that you are always on the lookout for the unusual, and deal with it properly when it enters your environment.

Let's consider the five distinct levels of awareness—the

Conditions of White, Yellow, Orange, Red and Black. Even though there are 5 levels, let's not feel overwhelmed about it as if we were studying for a U.S. Department of Homeland Security Threat Levels test. First, let's eliminate the easy ones—Conditions White and Black. White is while we're sleeping, and black is while we are in full panic mode. Sure— we should be aware that they exist, but we should never operate in those conditions during our day. Here is our chart outlining the levels, starting at Condition White.

AWARENESS ESCALTATION CHART

WHITE	Sleeping; unprepared to take action.
YELLOW	Prepared, alert & relaxed. Good situational awareness.
ORANGE	Alert to probable danger. Ready to take action.
RED	Action mode. Focused on the emergency at hand.
BLACK	Panic. Breakdown of physical & mental performance.

Condition White

This is the *tranquil* state of mind where we are mellow, comfortable, with no cares or worries. We sleep soundly, and our thoughts are light and steady.

Condition Yellow

In this the *aware* state of mind we are operating smoothly, and are up and moving around, aware of our surroundings and everything in our environment. Maybe I'm watching something on TV. If I hear a low pitch warning or alarm, I am instantly focused on it and ready to act. I may elevate my awareness to the next level—Orange. If a car pulls up in front of my house or if there is yelling in the neighborhood, I will take immediate notice and assess the situation.

Condition Orange

This is the *alert* condition. We know there is a chance that something might be dangerous, so we remain ready for action if we sense something. I take my small children to the mall or park and keep them very close and supervised, because I don't want them to get lost, kidnapped or hurt. I'm on the lookout for danger and ready to respond at a moment's notice. We should be in this condition most of the time. If we see something out of place, we can immediately move up to the next level—Condition Red.

Condition Red

This *constantly on your toes* state of mind is something I experienced constantly as a police officer patrolling the dodgy sections of North Las Vegas at night. Certainly, every raid with the SWAT Team had me in Condition Red. In Condition Red you are on the lookout for something; on your guard for danger, around every corner. A hunter is in Condition Red. You are the hunter. We are in Condition Red during many physical games in athletics. We assess the environment. We are actively looking for signs of danger or attack. We are in a defensive posture, looking for opportunities to go on offense. We are hypersensitive and hyperaware. We are ready to strike.

Condition Black is a Dangerous State of Mind

There is a *panic* state of mind that many of us have experienced, where time seems to slow and our brains seem to shrink into darkness as we struggle to get a handle on what is happening around us. It is a mental *lag-time*; the time it takes for us to wrap our brain around the event unfolding before us. It is a state of *denial*. We just don't want to believe that this is really happening. We are unprepared for the event—something has happened that we were not expecting, and our brain freezes and goes dark while we wrestle to figure out what it is and how to respond.

This lag-time in Condition Black is the *extra* time it takes your brain to:

1) recognize that something has occurred,

2) assess it, and

3) react to it in an appropriate manner.

Recognition, assessment and reaction are normal in every Condition, and each color level has its own timing for the three. The problem in Condition Black is that it's a dead zone—a period of inaction. This inaction can be devastating if real danger is present, and it is often real danger that prompts Condition Black.

A perfect example of Condition Black is illustrated in a short video produced by Fight Back Nation, which you can view at FightBackNation.org/video, titled, "Surviving an Active Shooter in the Workplace." In the 5-minute video a group of workers is sitting at a conference table discussing a business matter when loud pops ring out from somewhere in the building. Because the sounds are completely unexpected and out of context in this work environment, our brains tend to seek a classification for the sounds that makes better sense in this context. The reality that shots are being fired just 60 feet down the hall is something the brain doesn't want to accept, so it tries to suppress that probability while entertaining a host of other possibilities. Firecrackers, banging on a hard object, something fell, or inexplicable noises down the street all wrestle for predominance in the brain while the obvious cause is forced to remain unrecognized, unconscious, and unspoken. Everyone stares at one another in Condition Black, waiting for someone to offer a plausible explanation, while brains grow dark and close down to possibilities, convincing themselves that there is nothing seriously wrong. Although this may seem a little unlikely here in the light of day as we discuss active shooters, the reality is that this is the most frequent response to gunfire in the workplace or schoolhouse.

In short, when people hear *BOOM—BOOM—BOOM* they tend to freeze and spend precious time trying to decide if there's a problem or not. Through this conversation we are elevating your awareness, and helping to get you into a normal state of Condition Orange, so you are very aware of what is going on around you and on the lookout for danger or problems. The moment you hear the *BOOM* you move up into Condition Red and react appropriately.

Let's consider our possible response if we were in the county-sponsored employee training and Christmas party in San Bernardino. We might have been inside talking with coworkers when we saw two people enter dressed like SWAT Team members wearing ski masks and carrying AR style rifles. Although it is extremely out of place at a Christmas party, our minds go into the confused state of Condition Black. "That's strange. What does that have to do with Christmas? Is this another drill?" Our brain tries to convince us that there's a logical explanation for what we are seeing—an explanation that is not the obvious. We try to process the information while ignoring the very real probability that the information we are receiving is completely accurate and the story it conveys is "deadly attack." We resist the truth—the truth is unthinkable—we just don't want to believe it is happening. This is lag-time; Condition Black. In this state we waste a lot of time, allowing the shooter a greater opportunity to kill us and others.

Our resistance to the truth of what we see and hear is understandable. Most people simply do not grow up as I did in foreign embassies where we were on the constant lookout for attacks. Most people have not served in dangerous neighborhoods as police officers, or as members of SWAT Teams. I get it. However, because we live in a world where evil people kill others for the pure sport of it, it's my job to change the way you think about the world around you. There is a process of converting our conditioned thinking to a consistent Condition Orange—a constant state of heightened awareness.

In the case of the Christmas party in San Bernardino, let's say that I give you a call the day before the party, and I say, "Hey, you may remember when we used to work together. Now I'm working at Homeland Security on a counter-terrorism task force, and we're hearing chatter about a call for a lone wolf attack on a Christmas party somewhere in the western United States—especially if it's sponsored by a government entity. We have no idea if anyone is preparing such an attack, or where it might happen. I just wanted to let you know what I had heard. So pass this information on to others—especially those who attend government-sponsored Christmas parties."

Because we had the conversation, I elevated your status to Condition Orange—perhaps Condition Red. I encouraged you to be on the lookout, even if there is nothing specific in the warning. You are now aware of your surroundings, and keeping your eyes and ears open, especially as you enter the county employee Christmas party the next day. You speak to your friends at the party and share the information that I gave you. By sharing that information, their status is elevated to Condition Orange as well. If you put your finger here and go back a few pages, you'll recall that Condition Orange is a state of being very aware of all of the people and activities in your environment. It's not quite Condition Red, where you are ready to do battle or to spring into action at any moment. It is merely a heightened level awareness of what's going on around you, with the idea in the back of your mind that you need to exercise extreme caution if anything out of the ordinary presents itself. You are paying close attention and are prepared.

With the warning in the back of your mind you eat shrimp and drink a Dr. Pepper like everyone else, but you have looked around and made sure that everyone in attendance belongs there. You have noticed that the room you're in has three exits. You've made sure that your spouse is within reaching distance of you. Although you aren't ready to spring to attack, as in Condition Red, you're ready to react quickly to anything unusual. You notice the door opening and you see two people enter dressed in black body armor and ski masks carrying AR-15 rifles. While most of the others notice them out of the corner of their eye and their brains go into Condition Black as they attempt to make the unusual accessories and behavior fit into some sort of normal explanation, you slip immediately into Condition Red and reach out and grab your spouse's arm and the two of you slide quickly to the nearest exit, followed closely by those with whom you shared my warning earlier, and you signal the alarm for everyone to run and hide—or fight.

This is my purpose—to elevate your status to a constant Condition Orange, always prepared to elevate to Condition Red when necessary, and to keep you out of Condition Black, no matter what might happen. As a police officer and protection specialist, I try to plant the right seeds in the minds of my trainees, and readers, to elevate them to a constant Condition Orange—ready to elevate to Condition Red the second they see something that informs them there is danger. Our trainees don't become paranoid as a result of our training. In fact, because we give them the tools they need to survive a dangerous situation, the paranoia they used to carry around worrying about their classroom or office being invaded by a sick shooter, dissipates and becomes Condition Orange—they are always aware of what is happening in their environment, and ready to recognize and assess those things that appear to be out of place. Soon, they adopt our mantra; **Prepared, not Paranoid**.

Your Condition Level—In Dangerous Situations

There's a beautiful waterfall a little upstream from Provo, Utah near Sundance called Bridal Veil Falls. It's such a popular name for a waterfall that I sometimes wonder if every state has one. This particular waterfall is over 600 feet tall and eventually splashes into the gorgeous Provo River below. It's an incredible site to take families and loved ones to visit, and people flock there by the thousands each year to stand a few feet from the raging river to feed the fish in the pool at the bottom of the waterfall and take in the sight. If a child were to fall into the river at this location during the Spring runoff, they would have little chance of survival. Knowing this, and seeing it when they arrive, all of those parents still take their children to see the falls and the fish. The same can be said of thousands of sites around America, and many thousands more around the world.

So why is it that parents are so laid back about taking themselves and their children to a place where death and heartache are only a slip on a wet rock away? In this case the parents *recognize* the danger, they *assess* what they must do to protect their children from it, and they *react* by putting themselves between their children and the river, or by keeping everyone a safe distance from the danger.

We live in a dangerous world. Taking proper precautions and reacting appropriately when danger rears its head is what has kept billions of us alive from the very beginning. The more we can train ourselves to be in Condition Red when appropriate, and use our wits, our training and our Warrior DNA, the better our chances of surviving. This is especially true when dangerous people put themselves in our path.

Chapter Five — Be Prepared

Prepare and Be Aware

Interestingly, the nation of Brazil has much stricter gun laws, but is many times more violent than the U.S. Unlike the U.S. they had for many years been spared the experience of a school mass shooting—until recently. I received a phone call and was asked to come to Brazil to be the keynote speaker on Active Shooter and Mass Shootings at a three-day national security conference held in São Paulo. In Brazil the 'malls' are particularly vulnerable to criminal and other attacks. It is unknown to most Americans that the malls in Brazil are extremely high-end. Only the wealthiest in their society can afford to shop there, which makes the malls an attractive target.

Because of their high-end patrons, the Brazilian malls have armed security, trained in how to respond to robberies or gang related activities. But after the first school mass shooting in over 20 years occurred, they all worried that something similar could happen on their mall property, if someone decided to make a political or social statement. They now wanted to know how to fortify and prepare in case of a mass shooting in their facilities. Of course, many who were responsible for the safety of hospitals, public buildings and schools were concerned and in attendance. In the U.S. we had suffered mass shootings in nightclubs and theaters, so they were paying very close attention to the strategies and information I was sharing.

Dave Acosta providing a training session for Brazilian SWAT Team members.

As we discussed their unique issues, I related how I had recently listened to a television report that said the local Walmart had only two exits, resulting in a trap for customers in the event of a mass shooter. I shared how I was perplexed about that news report, because it simply isn't true. I went to my local Walmart store and walked through it quickly, counting at least 14 exits. The same is true of malls—there are numerous exits, and some stores in the mall have their own private exit. Most grocery stores have employee exits, as well as loading areas. All of these can be accessed in the event of an active shooter. Although I am always well aware of the existence and placement of exits wherever I find myself, it occurs to me that most people just don't realize that most buildings, especially shopping locations, have several points of exit. Therefore, one of my recommendations to the mall owners was to be sure to clearly mark the exits in their malls and train employees on how to guide patrons to these exits during a critical incident.

Your New Worldview

Once you've read this book or received our training, you are different, and will now notice the exits wherever you are. You will see the world differently than before. You will not go into Condition Black in an emergency, but will go into Condition Red—like a momma bear ready to protect her young. I want you to be conscious of your surroundings, wherever you are. If you're home, think about what you would do if a bad guy suddenly appeared. I don't want you to be paranoid about it—I want you to be prepared. I want you to think it through—to the point that a bad guy who decides to enter your home has made the biggest mistake of his life. I want you to walk the possible exits of the buildings where you spend most of your time, and plan your primary and secondary escape route. I want you to pay attention every time you enter a new place—grocery store, church, mall, school, restaurant, business, etc. Know where the exits are, and where they lead. Get a quick feel for who should be there, and notice if someone appears who doesn't fit. Notice what people are doing, and watch their body language. Open your eyes, and your mind will follow.

As you become more observant of your surroundings, your situational awareness improves, and you begin to notice more in the world around you generally. At the point that you begin to consciously assess the world around you, generally in a heightened state of awareness, Condition Orange, things that you had usually missed before now, become more a part of your everyday life. The greenness of the grass, your neighbor playing with the dog or who walks through your neighborhood or near your car. People just don't look up and look around until they are trained to 'notice' what's going on in the room. We teach our trainees that there is a big difference between paranoid and prepared—and we help them become prepared.

Recap

We've discussed how to **run** from an active shooter—have a first route of escape, and secondary route of escape already in mind. Wherever you work or go to school or church— you have a primary and a secondary route in mind, where you will run if you hear an active shooter. When you get far enough away that you're out of immediate danger, call 9-1-1 and describe the shooter and the weapons he has.

If There is No Escape

As part of your preparation, in every location where you spend any amount of time, know what you'll do if there is no escape route. If you can't **run** away from the danger, **take cover** behind something that will stop a bullet. Something like a brick wall, concrete planter or heavy wooden furniture you can get behind. If you can't get behind something that will stop bullets, then **concealment** includes objects you can hide behind, although they won't stop a bullet. Anything that will block the shooter's view of you will do—a closet door, a large desk or even a curtain. In most cases, he'll be looking for the obvious, exposed targets.

Fight Back

Without specific training, *how to fight* is a completely subjective concept. In the event we are physically confronted by a mass shooter, and we can't immediately escape, we have just one option—fight. There are no more options. We can die, or we can fight. Statistically, fighting back works. There is no doubt, and there is no argument—it simply works. As I've said, in most cases 99 percent of the people present during a Mass Shooting have no firearm, so Fight Back Nation provides simple defensive techniques to fight back against a shooter. I know when most people think about learning to fight back against an armed lunatic, they think long-term self-defense courses are necessary—and it becomes a non-starter for most people. That won't be necessary. In our training sessions we inevitably end up teaching smaller women to disarm larger men in just about an hour of training. Again, you can learn the fundamentals of Run—Hide—Fight by watching our 5-minute Active Shooter video at FightBackNation.org/video. We also have and **The Inside Leverage Takeaway** disarming technique video there, where you can learn the simple technique in a step-by-step demonstration.

I hear about school districts directing teachers and students to throw books and other objects at mass shooters. It's hard to emphasize just how ineffective that idea is—or how dangerous it is. I can tell you from experience that throwing a book at a psychopath with a gun in his hands is an invitation to shoot you first, before you can throw another one. You may hurt him a little with a book or other object you throw, but you are not preventing/stopping further action (shooting). Even if a lot of people are throwing things at the shooter, it will not disrupt his ability to shoot and kill them. The only time we recommend throwing 'anything' at a shooter is if it is as a distraction, followed immediately by a counter attack.

Some schools and organizations instruct their staff to pick up whatever they can, like a chair, and hit the shooter. Truthfully, that's a much better solution than throwing items, but still not the most effective way stop him. We need to disrupt his ability to continue to shoot and kill innocent people. A physical attack needs to impede his actions, so you must disarm him or wrestle him physically to the ground until help arrives.

What if the entire room of people rush him at once and beat him, or hit him with chairs or books, or stab him with pens? Your chances of subduing him and surviving are much better if you do that—because it stops him from walking around and shooting people at will. However, training a classroom of children to attack a crazed shooter is just not practical at all. Let's give the teachers the tools and techniques needed to effectively attack and disarm the shooter. That's what we do at Fight Back Nation.

Learn How to Fight

So many teachers and school staff are initially very skeptical about any sort of fighting back technique when they hear about us, and many hesitate to join us for training. They are usually required to attend by the administration, and I estimate that a full 10 percent of the attendees at our training sessions are resistant toward us in the beginning, if not actually physically sick because they are compelled to be there. I feel only empathy for them. It's not fair that a person who already gives so much of herself to take on other people's children all day—giving and giving and giving, so that each young person can become prepared for life—should have to worry about a mass shooter coming into her classroom and murdering her students.

There is simply nothing fair in it. I understand that teachers don't want to have this subject forced onto them. They are terrified to even think about and discuss a mass shooter coming into their classroom. Then over the course of the next two hours, I see them transform from frightened, powerless victims to empowered momma bears, able and willing to defend themselves and their students if the need ever arises. They routinely come up to me or members of our training staff after the training and tell us how relieved they are—how their secret dark burden has been lifted—how their fear has transformed to empowerment. I really can't describe how this make us feel! It's incredibly rewarding.

Because we are empowering teachers and staff in schools, they are no longer plagued by the constant fear of 'what if it happens today?' They are prepared. Our training gives them peace of mind—something that the terror of school shootings had robbed from them. Their focus is back on teaching. If anything happens, they will be frightened, like anyone would, but they will know what to do to protect themselves and those they cherish. They won't feel powerless, because they won't be powerless. Many teachers, staff members, administrators and professors have now become volunteers, and show up with us at training sessions, demonstrating what to do and how to do it. Some of our volunteer instructors are police officers, US military veterans and even active duty Navy SEALs.

Fighting Someone Holding a Gun

The rifle seems more ominous, but in an up close encounter, it is much harder for the shooter to retain control of the rifle when you use the **Inside Leverage Takeaway** disarming technique.

The handgun is smaller, and has about half the magazine capacity as a rifle. It is pretty inaccurate at distances over 30 feet. This is especially true of a moving target—so anyone moving quickly presents a much more difficult target to hit. Our Inside Leverage Takeaway technique has proven very effective with handguns too. Semi-automatic handguns eject the spent casing from the gun after every shot as the slide goes to the back of the gun and then pushes a new round into the firing position as the slide returns to the forward position. If you are wrestling the handgun away from the shooter, and use the over hand (hand over the slide) technique we teach, you will prevent the gun from cycling in a new round if the gun were to go off during the fight. Because you have prevented the slide from going back after the first shot, the gun was unable to eject the spent casing and replace it with a new bullet. After that first shot, the gun is no longer "hot" or ready to fire. To reload it, the shooter would have to regain control of the pistol and yank the slide all the way back. That's why it is so important for you to stay in the fight until someone helps subdue him—you are preventing him from reloading and shooting anyone else. Every second you are wrestling him is a second that he is not shooting children or others. Keep in mind, these shooters are acutely aware of the small window of opportunity they have as the 3 minutes tick down.

Some mass shooters have a pipe bomb or other explosive device, but not often. Get away as fast as possible if you see him take one out. Distance and putting cover between you and the explosive device are the two most important things you can do. If you had to choose between distance and cover, get as far away as possible. If you believe there is an explosive device present during an active shooter incident, make sure at the first opportunity to share that information with the police. Include location and a description of the device.

The body count record for mass shootings in a school environment is Virginia Tech. His weapon was handguns. They are the least accurate choice and have the smallest ammo capacity. Notwithstanding, he was able to kill 32, most of whom were in an age group and level of fitness that they were very capable of fighting back and defending themselves. It is ironic and sad that most of them didn't know that they could fight back against the attack. One student tried, Air Force Cadet Mathew La Porte, but his path to the shooter was in the direct line of fire and he was quickly cut down. Almost all of the rest sought to run, which is always the first, best choice. However, because most of them were in college classrooms with just one door, which the shooter stood in front of as he fired, the only place to go was against the far wall. The shooter was at liberty to simply walk among the huddled students, and shoot them at will. When he ran out of ammunition, he would walk back out to the hallway and reach into his duffle bag where he kept preloaded magazines. He popped them into his handguns, and walked back into the classroom and continued the carnage where he left off a minute before, uninterrupted by anyone. The shooter was a tiny little weak college student. He would have been vulnerable to a counter attack—especially when he was returning to the hallway for more ammo. This lesson must never be lost. We MUST fight back! Failing to attack the shooter when he runs out of ammo is a missed opportunity to stop the carnage and survive.

The Guy With The Gun Isn't in Control — He Doesn't Win

We all must change the way we think. As things are, culturally, the guy with the gun is in control. We all do what the guy with the gun says. When the guy with the gun starts shooting, we run as far as we can, which in many cases ends at a wall, then we stop, and wait to see what he does. Because he has the gun, he projects the illusion that he is in control. It is only an illusion, fueled by the false premise that the gun is all-powerful. The gun does all the talking. The gun decides. If we change the way we think, we take back control.

A Shooter is Vulnerable Everywhere, Except Where He's Aiming

A shooter can only shoot one person at a time. He can only shoot in one direction at a time. No one wants to be the one being shot at—but the reality is that if the shooter is aiming at you to shoot you, you have nothing to lose by grabbing his gun and directing it away from your body.

If he's not aiming his gun at you in this moment, he likely will get to you soon; so you **must** attack! As long as the shooter is left to pick off his victims one at a time, without interference, he is in Condition Red, because this is what he anticipated. He will empty his magazines, then go reload, then empty them again, and again. All of this uninterrupted by his victims. This is his plan, and he assumes it will go smoothly until the police arrive—at which point he will give up or die. He is *expecting* that everyone will try to run away from him, will huddle together, and will wait until he gets to them. To him, this is like a video game where he walks around and shoots as many frightened victims as he can in 3 to 5 minutes. There will be no resistance. That is his only plan. As soon as someone interferes with him and his shooting-at-will process, it disrupts up his plan—it stops his process. Because he hadn't counted on this, his brain will quickly plunge him into Condition Black, where his physical and mental faculties begin to fail him.

This shooter has never committed mass murder. He is not

trained to overcome a counter attack or adapt to the unpredictable. He is not expecting your attack—your resistance. A 110-pound teacher suddenly wedging herself between him and his gun is the last thing he expected. He is suddenly as helpless as everyone else in the building, and the best he can do is fight with his hands—just like everyone else. Only now, he is greatly outnumbered. What happens when a mass shooter is interrupted? He usually runs or shoots himself. He may run for a backup weapon in his bag—so hold him; wrestle with him if you have to, but don't let him get back to his bag. If interrupted, he may run out of the building in an attempt to escape. If he stays there, law enforcement officers will be on the scene shortly, so control him if possible.

Rush the Shooter and Grab the Gun

If the shooter aims to the right and you are to the left in close proximity, or in the front, you must rush him and grab the gun. Because he can only shoot in one direction at a time, at any given moment he is vulnerable from almost every direction.

Use **The Inside Leverage Takeaway** disarming technique to put yourself between him and the gun and disarm him. If you do not immediately disarm the shooter, stay in the fight. Never give up. You may not realize it, because you've never been in the circumstance (as the shooter has not), but if you have something in your hand and someone grabs it, you cannot use that item effectively during the fight. Try it with something. Hold a large plastic utensil in your hand, or a stick, or something approximating a handgun or rifle, and tell someone to take it away from you as—as if their life depends on it. You'll instantly see that your ability to use the object effectively is critically impeded. Plus, snatching the tool or weapon away from the person holding it is much easier than most people realize. Getting your hands on it and wrestling the person for control of it is really very effective. And don't forget—every second that he spends wrestling with you for control of the gun is a person that's not being shot. So if you're not in the direct line of fire and you are close enough, rush him and grab the gun.

Something that most people don't realize is that people are powerless to not blink if something is thrown toward their face. If you feel you are a little too far away from the shooter to rush him without him getting a shot off at you, grab anything you can find and throw it at his head. His natural "lizard brain" triggers an involuntary reaction that will force him to close his eyes prior to impact. As he flinches, you rush him and grab the gun. You can cover 20 feet in the time it takes him to recover from his flinch. Again, this doesn't mean that you should throw things at an active shooter to stop him or hurt him. That will merely make you his next target. I mean throw something at his face to distract him only long enough to rush him and grab his gun. It may not be something that you prefer to do, but if people are being shot that close to you, your turn is coming soon— so this is your best chance of surviving, and saving many others in the process.

The Disarming Technique

The Inside Leverage Takeaway disarming technique works. I recently showed it to some self-defense professionals—a retired Green Beret and a professional MMA fighter—and handed them the plastic orange pistol and AR rifle, and told them to keep me from disarming them. I was able to demonstrate the disarming technique effectively and it was at that point that they asked me to slow it down and walk them through the process step by step. I showed them the move in slow motion, and they both saw how simple it was, and agreed it is the best disarming technique they've ever seen.

Just to get their opinion about hitting the shooter, I asked them if, with their training and ability, they could strike an armed shooter, with a fist or an object, and stop him. They both said it would take more luck than skill to do it successfully. Hitting or striking the shooter is simply unproductive. Low probability, high risk.

A teacher practices The Inside Leverage Takeaway disarming technique.

If Run or Hide aren't viable options for you, then you must Fight, and **The Inside Leverage Takeaway** disarming technique is simply the easiest and most effective method to do that. Let's look at it now.

First, as we've said, get out of sight of the shooter if possible, so when you do ambush him, you have the element of surprise on your side. If you can lock the door and barricade it, do that. A gunman making it in past a locked and barricaded door is highly unlikely. This means get behind a door, barricade it with a couch or desk lengthwise that someone holds in place if possible, and turn off the lights. When he enters a dimly lit room from a well-lit environment, it takes a few seconds for his eyes to adjust. This is the time for you to attack!

However, if you are in a room that does not have a locking door or a room like a public bathroom where there is no door, get around the side or corner of the entry. Position yourself at a 90-degree angle from the direction he must enter, and get ready to ambush him from the side with **The Inside Leverage Takeaway** disarming technique. He will be surprised and his brain will instantly go to Condition Black. Let's bullet point those:

- Close the door and lock it
- Barricade door with a couch or desk or other large heavy object
- Have someone lie on the floor and hold the furniture in place
- Turn off the lights
- Get to the side of the doorway at a 90-degree angle
- Ambush from 90 degree angle using **Inside Leverage Takeaway**

When we do trainings in schools and workplaces we send our people through the building where teachers and staff are waiting to ambush them. The teachers and employees do all of the above, and successfully disarm the shooter—every time.

Again, you can learn the simple **Inside Leverage Takeaway** disarming technique in a short step-by-step demonstration video that we have put on our website at FightBackNation.org/video. Please watch it, then practice it with everyone that you care about.

The 5 minute video explains how to survive a mass shooting in the workplace.

Chapter Six — Making School Shootings Unproductive

The Columbine Tragedy

In April 1999, Eric Harris and Dylan Klebold embarked on a murderous rampage in their own high school, killing 12 students and one teacher, and wounding 21. It was 45 minutes before the shooters were confirmed dead.

Columbine changed everything. It changed how law enforcement thinks about and responds to mass shootings, and how schools do too. I was a young SWAT officer in North Las Vegas when Columbine happened, and our immediate discussions were about the 45-minute time gap between the first call and getting to the shooters, whom they found deceased. It's important to recognize that officers acted heroically within that timeframe. They were following their protocols, running into the school, rescuing frightened and wounded kids. They did absolutely everything they had been trained to do, saving lives in spite of the murderous rampage.

Following Columbine, however, law enforcement re-trained everyone, and the policy is now much different. Now, when the call goes out that there is an Active Shooter at a school, or other facility, every law enforcement officer of every type within the area knows it's his or her duty to get to the shooter as quickly as humanly possible and terminate the threat. It's that simple. My daughter is a police officer with the local city police department near me. She knows that if the call comes across that there is an active shooter, she is to drop whatever she is doing and rush as fast as possible to the scene, and with other arriving officers, move quickly to the location of the shooter.

If an FBI agent is on his way to an investigation and the Active Shooter call goes out, it's the same for him. He is to rush as fast as possible to the scene, and with any other officer he meets there, immediately move to the location of the shooter and engage him. In some cases in more rural areas where officers may be arriving one at a time with a significant time gap for backup, they will go in anyway and engage the shooter.

In a recent false alarm in my county, two officers were at the location and hunting the suspected active shooter in less than one minute. By the time they radioed "all clear," there were over 30 officers at the scene, and by the time they were cleared to return to duty there were over 100 officers at the scene. This is in a rural community—not a large city with a huge force. These officers were pouring in from all surrounding areas to assist. That's how far law enforcement has come in their training and commitment that not one extra round is fired at an innocent victim by a deranged mass shooter. Young police officers are now graduating from the police academy with more active shooter training than we possessed when I was an active SWAT team member. They are aggressive and ready to fight the evil face to face. It's inspiring to see them spring into action and become unstoppable hunters on a moment's notice.

Because of this new law enforcement dynamic, innocent

people at mass shootings only have to fend off the active shooter for a couple of minutes. The shooter knows his time is extremely limited. He will be looking to shoot as many easy targets as he can in that short amount of time. Because classroom doors in K—12 schools lock, a mass shooter will likely not bother trying to get into a locked classroom, but will move quickly to an area where he believes he will find easy targets in the open. Therefore, every classroom door should have a lock on it, and every teacher should lock it during a lockdown. Many people worry that a mass shooter will merely shoot the lock on a classroom door and enter it. Although that's possible, shooting a lock off a door and making entry is very difficult to do and as of the writing of this book, I cannot confirm a single incident where the shooter has successfully done this. It has never been done. Shooters have always looked for the easiest targets.

In one case a shooter shot through a door being held closed by college students. The rounds penetrated the door hitting the students on the other side, driving them back, allowing the shooter to make entry into the classroom. That's why we train our teachers and others to barricade the door with something from inside the room, and lay behind it on the ground to reinforce it.

A mass shooter also won't expect any resistance, and anyone who counterattacks or uses any sort of defensive move will surprise the shooter, and he can often be quickly overcome.

Never Hide in Restrooms

Bathrooms in schools and office buildings (and the theater, the mall, the store, etc.) nearly always have just one entry/exit into the room—which may not even have a door. If a child or someone else runs to hide in a restroom, there is simply no place to hide, and no way to escape, and he will be trapped and an easy target. Mass shooters who run out of easy targets often head to the restrooms where they know there will be people with nowhere to run or hide and no way to barricade. We always train teachers and supervisors to check the restrooms on their way out of the building to ensure no student or potential victim is hiding inside. Anyone who isn't in the direct line of fire and doesn't have immediate responsibility for children should run to the restrooms to ensure that no children have hidden inside.

Dave Acosta speaking on Fight Back techniques at the Utah County Sherriff's Teacher Academy.

If you do get trapped in a restroom, find the first 90 degree angle and prepare to ambush the shooter and aggressively counter attack him as he enters.

If the restroom has a door that only opens inward and does not lock, you can try to block his entry by getting one or more of you on the floor just in front of the door and putting your feet against the door with your legs outstretched in front of you to act as a doorstop. If it helps, lie flat on the floor and outstretch your arms against something for added resistance. It's your best chance of keeping the shooter out. Either way, be sure to get low to the floor. Don't forget to turn off the lights if you can. A shooter who encounters a human doorstop assumes someone is on the other side blocking him, and he may shoot through the door to eliminate the person. If he does so and nothing changes, chances are he will just move on. If he is able to force his way in, have someone ready to ambush him as he enters and his eyes are adjusting to the dark.

Aftermath

We train teachers what to do after an active shooter situation. Even when they have successfully placed their students safely behind a locked door and the police arrived within a couple of minutes, there will be a lockdown period when officials go through the campus to clear every room and ensure that any wounded have received appropriate care. Teachers should be prepared to be in lockdown with the students for up to three hours. Therefore, they should be prepared with a sufficient supply of water, improvised toilet facilities with a privacy barrier and basic medical supplies including a tourniquet and gauze pads. In our seminars we train teachers and administrators what to stock and how to use it.

It's Time For Standard Protocols In U.S. Schools

America has not had a fire related death in a school since 1952. The U.S. has national protocols and fire drills, all mandated; and it works. Schools have frequent fire drills, and everyone knows what to do in case of a fire. No one dies from a school fire. Although the nation went to work immediately following the tragedy at Columbine and changed its law enforcement agency protocols to match the particular challenge, schools have not. The only standard that has been accepted across the country is the very basic RUN – HIDE – FIGHT response to an active shooter. This very basic response protocol is very subjective in its application from school district to school district. That means that law enforcement agencies that have more than one school district in their jurisdiction, may be responding to a variety of schools with different response plans. This means responding officers may not know what to expect from school to school as it relates to their protocols. It really is time that we standardize the protocols for schools to prepare for mass shooting events.

RED CARD System

Fight Back Nation has adopted a previously developed, simple system to help law enforcement identify which class-rooms have immediate need of medical attention as they move through the school during an active shooter crisis or in the aftermath. Each classroom is equipped with some basic supplies, including a red card, which can be slid under the door during the crisis to identify the presence of a person in need of immediate medical assistance. Even if police officers can't stop and help, they can easily get on their radio and identify that classroom as having a medical emergency. Dispatch will immediately inform subsequent rescue teams of the locations where medical attention is needed.

Hall Boss

RUN – HIDE – FIGHT means that your first choice in an emergency should be run away from the danger. However, the problem is that if the **fire alarm** sounds and all of the offices or classrooms suddenly empty into the hallway, we have just created a target rich environment for a shooter. We call this a *fatal funnel*. If this were the case, a mass shooter would simply go into a school and pull the fire alarm or start a fire, filling the fatal funnel instantly. In that circumstance hundreds of children would be pouring into the hallway with the alarms sounding, and it would be quite difficult to see and hear that the shooter is killing students.

Instead, when the alarm sounds, teachers should pause and look out into the hallways, in both directions, to first confirm that there is not an active shooter present. Most classrooms lead to hallways that exit to an outside door. In our HALL BOSS system, each teacher goes to the classroom door and looks out into the hallway to ensure the hallway is clear. The teacher can be careful, looking quickly at first, then taking a longer look in both directions. The two teachers at the end of the hallway near the doors that lead outside hurry to the exit door and one of them steps outside cautiously observing the environment, ensuring that there is no shooter waiting for the students to pour through the doors. When the two teachers are confident that there is no danger lurking outside the doors, they step back inside and give a thumbs up to the rest of the teachers watching from their doorways down the hall. All of the teachers signal thumbs up then instruct their students to file quickly into the hallway and proceed to the outer exit doors. This extra level of security costs no more than 15 or 20 seconds, yet it is a safe way to ensure that all of those children are getting quickly away from the danger.

The Dispatch Call

A typical 911 call to emergency dispatch goes like this:

911: "911. What's your emergency?"

CALLER: "My neighbor's dog is barking again, and I need to sleep because I have to work in the morning."

911: "Okay. We'll send an officer out when someone is available."

The dispatcher types this information into the system and it will come up in the dispatch system queue, and when officers have made their way down the list of priorities, the next one available will go check on the barking dog problem.

The 911 active shooter call goes more like this:

911: "911. What's your emergency?"

CALLER: "There's an active shooter at our school!"

Instead of simply talking to the caller, the dispatcher will say aloud for the supervisor to hear: "You have an active shooter at your school? What school?"

At this point, a supervisor comes to the dispatcher and monitors the call, and as the dispatcher types the information into the system as a top priority call, the supervisor has the ability to go live on a law enforcement common channel, who announces to all agencies at once, "Stand by, we have an active shooter at Treeline Middle School. Stand by for details." Some systems have a tone that precedes all common channel emergency announcements, like three beeps.

Every law enforcement officer that receives notices on the common channel immediately knows there is an active shooter at that school, and he or she drops everything and drives to Treeline Middle School as fast as possible. Some officers will be very close by simple happenstance, and others will be farther away. Any details about the number of shooters and weapons used will be provided *en route*, and the first officer on the scene does his best to ascertain the situation and the location of the shooter as he arrives and runs full speed toward the shooter. Some jurisdictions dictate that the first officer on the scene await the arrival of a backup officer, but even in those jurisdictions a second officer usually arrives within mere seconds of the first.

No Longer Productive

With this understanding of how law enforcement has narrowed the response time to under three minutes, often less than one minute, teachers and staff have a much better understanding of their role in preserving their own lives and those of the students in the event of an active shooter on campus.

With the school mass-shooting window of time being so constricted by law enforcement's rapid response time, the appeal of schools as a "soft target" is diminishing proportionately. As I told the young Fox News affiliate reporter at the Sutherland Springs First Baptist Church scene, these shootings will stop when they are no longer productive. By severely restricting the amount of time a shooter has to shoot people at will, and by teaching educational professionals how to actively defend against and even disarm an active shooter, many schools are simply not soft targets any longer. They are making themselves 'unproductive' targets.

When a school has 80 percent or more of its teachers and staff trained by Fight Back Nation, the school becomes a Fight Back Nation Certified School. We provide a large poster from Fight Back Nation that announces to everyone that the school has been trained to fight back against an active shooter, and is not a 'soft target.' The large poster says:

FIGHT BACK

NATION
CERTIFIED SCHOOL

We are a FIGHT BACK NATION Certified School. Teachers, Administrators and Support Staff are trained and prepared to protect all students, and will use whatever force necessary to deter and stop any persons who enter with ill intentions.

Because school shooters are looking for soft targets that will offer no resistance, a school with our large poster hanging in the entry enjoys a layer of hardening protection that makes them 'unproductive' to a mass shooter. In other words, it warns the shooter that he is going to get a fight if he tries to shoot up this school. That's the last thing a school shooter wants. So receiving our training and having our certification poster hanging in the school has a double benefit—it has a preemptive benefit and makes the school an undesirable target, and it has a defensive benefit, in case the shooter can't read very well.

Dave presenting a Utah Charter School with their Fight Back Nation Certified poster. These posters hang at the front entrance of the schools for all to see.

The response of parents who see the poster has been overwhelmingly positive. Parents speak to the school administrators and express their confidence and relief that the school has become trained to defend their children in the event of an active shooter. As a result, schools are not just posting their Certification in the entry, but are posting it online, and on all of their social media accounts—announcing to the world that they are not a soft target.

Understanding Real Terrorism

I consider all mass shooters terrorists—because their goal is to strike fear into the hearts of the general population, and get us to change our behaviors based on their acts; *e.g.,* following a terrorist attack in a public location, parents don't send their kids to school or no one goes to the mall, theater, store, etc. There are dedicated terrorists, whose major goal in life is to make us afraid to do the normal things that underlie our culture and society. These are evil people, focused on destroying America one terror act at a time. To help us better understand this enemy, I invited my friend, Navy SEAL Omar Vieira, Naval Special Warfare Officer with the U.S. Navy to share his special insights. Omar is a terror hunter, with 22 years of active service, 15 of which have been in a command position. Omar knows the enemy, and has gone on hundreds of missions (I grossly understated his real world tactical experience) of the type that took out Osama bin Laden.

Omar is a friendly, kind, peaceful man. You wouldn't know that he is an elite Navy SEAL if you were to meet him at church or in the grocery store. But because he understands terrorists so profoundly, he has developed a basic philosophy, fundamental to understanding and overcoming the threat of terrorism.

"Violent people require a violent response."

Omar shares a brief description of the terrorist mindset for us, so we know what we're up against:

There is simply no other way to deal with a terrorist. They know only violence, and will not stop unless stopped by violence. Don't misunderstand me when I talk about terrorists. I'm not talking about non-terrorists. For instance, we know that Islamic Terrorists are responsible for tens of thousands of deaths around the globe every year. That doesn't mean that 90 percent of Muslims aren't perfectly peaceful. The problem is that the other 10 percent—of 1.8 billion—are somewhat supportive of global jihad. Therefore, we need to be aware, and be prepared. Terrorists are actively fighting a political and religious/cultural war in their own minds. To them, there is no *live and let live*—our lifestyle is an unholy affront to them, and they suffer under the mistaken belief that their god demands that they eliminate us in any way possible. It's their sacred duty to kill us—all of us. In their minds, there is no gray—everything is black or white to them. Again, we are talking about terrorists—those who have made a commitment to strike out in terror.

Those who come into the U.S. from the Middle East to strike with terror—there is no helping them; no getting them counseling to get over their misplaced anger. You can only stop them with death. It's sad, and almost inconceivable in our culture—but it's true. Perhaps those who have been raised here in America have a small chance of being reasoned with, or shown how wrong terrorism is. Unfortunately, we're talking about two-percent of radicalized Americans. Ninety-eight percent fit into the prior category.

Most terrorists are groomed for years to think a certain way. They are taught to hate Americans, hate Christianity, hate Jews and to hate all foreigners. Older 'handlers' take in directionless kids and indoctrinate them, grooming them and brainwashing them for years, eventually convincing them that the exchange of their life for a handful of others' lives is a good and holy trade.

Therefore, once a terror operation begins, there is no stopping it through normal tactics, like negotiation. There is no shouting "Halt!" and getting them to rethink their actions. They already have what they believe to be the upper hand, and they will complete their mission, no matter what happens. They are already dead in their own minds, and they have one foot in heaven already. If you hear them shout "Allahu Akbar!" you will see them follow through with violence, and the only way to stop the damage or even mitigate it is to resist them with violence. There is simply no reasoning with them and no stopping the carnage short of counter-attacking.

This is why I endorse Fight Back Nation. The teacher who is plagued with a feeling of hopelessness—that is exactly the goal of the terrorist. They want you to cower in the corner. They do not want or anticipate any resistance—no violence back to them. In the SEAL teams we train like we fight, doing it over and over again so that it is completely natural for us. We utilize the correct tools and equipment, to ensure we have the upper hand. Fight Back Nation provides average people with the training necessary to survive a mass shooter attack. Mass shooters, and terrorists alike—I've never seen one with the kind of training that really prepares them for when victims decide to fight back and immediately shut down the attack. They count on the submissive participation of their victims. You absolutely have to fight back.

— Omar Vieira

As I've learned in my own experience, and as we learn from Omar, terrorists are never looking to negotiate or give up when the pressure gets too high. They intend to inflict as much damage as they can until they are physically stopped. Beyond killing innocent children and citizens, terrorists are looking to extend their attack to include a drawn out battle with the authorities—the representatives of the evil government they are attacking. The last thing a terrorist expects during such an attack is to be tackled, counter-attacked, by his civilian victims. It stops them, just like it stops a school shooter—just like they were stopped on Flight

93. As Omar pointed out, most terrorists are not highly trained and sophisticated—this is especially true of the 'home-grown' variety. They have received a small amount of preparation—barely enough to carry out their specific attack. Resistance is something they are not prepared for. We take advantage of that weakness and counter-attack, just like we counter-attack a mass shooter of any type.

PHOTOS

Dave explaining the vulnerabilities of the grip on a handgun as he prepares to teach disarming techniques.

Teachers watch intently as Dave prepares to demonstrate the Inside Leverage Takeaway disarming technique at full speed.

A small teacher rips an AR15 from a Fight Back Nation instructor during a training session using the Inside Leverage Takeaway.

Speaking to a group of citizens about Active Shooter and how to survive. Utah County

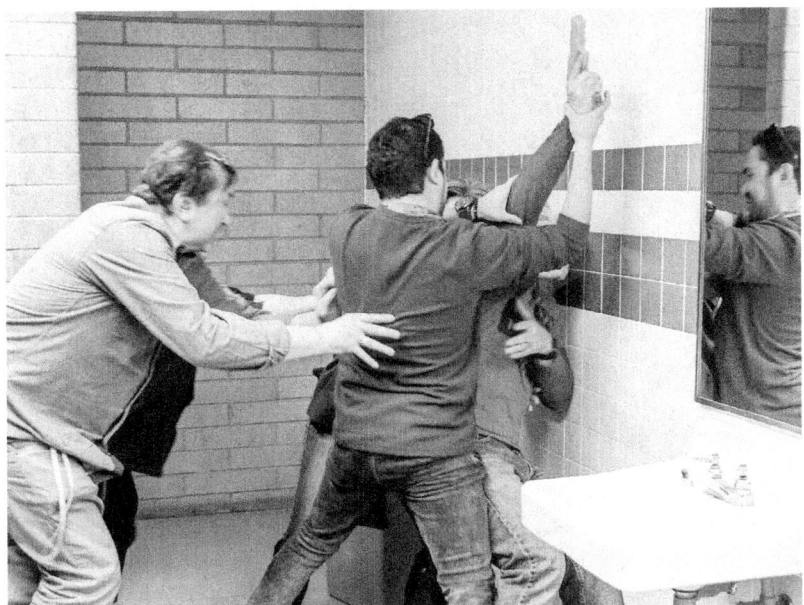

Teachers attack "would be" shooter as he enters a bathroom during a Fight Back Nation training session.

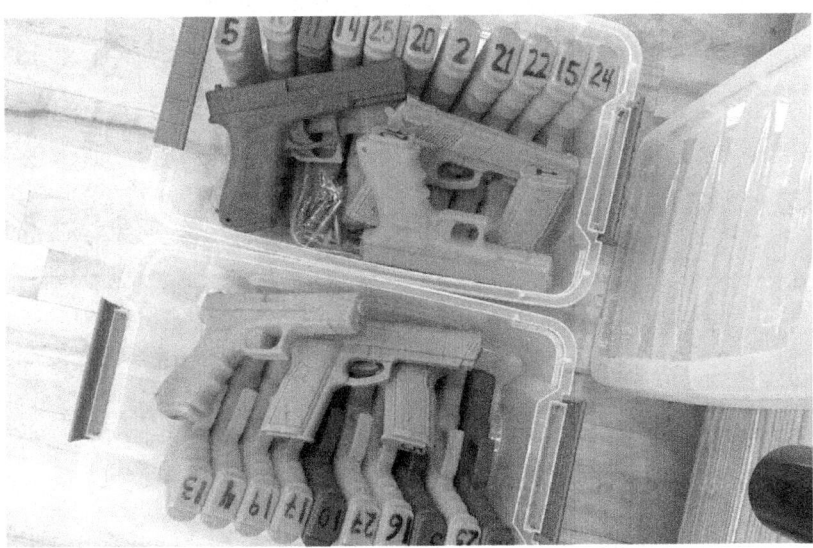

Plastics training weapons are provided as props for the training sessions.

Dave explaining and demonstrating how to gain inside leverage while counter attacking from the front of the shooter.

Fight Back Nation is busy providing training for corporations, schools, local businesses and even community events.

Teachers learning how to use the Inside Leverage Takeaway during a
Fight Back Nation training session.

Dave explaining the advantage of counter attacks from a 90 degree angle
at the entrance of a classroom.

Chapter Seven — A New Tool in the Fight

In 2008 I was quite occupied traveling around the world as a security consultant and contractor, setting up tactical and security systems and protocols for a wide variety of clients. As often happened, the president of a country asked me to come and assess his security team and systems. He felt they had a third-world security force, and he asked us to elevate them to a level of respectable proficiency and professionalism. This was something I found I was doing more often, because these were truly turbulent times, especially in Africa, South and Central America and Mexico.

One thing I noted was that the president had commissioned a new SUV to be converted to an armored vehicle. I thought that was a very good idea, and the upgrade work was done by a company that I worked with quite often. I asked the president's drivers to show me how they handled certain situations, and found the same thing I often did—the drivers were driving the armored vehicles the same way they used to drive regular SUVs. The problem with that, of course, is that all of the armor and upgrades add a lot of weight to the vehicle, and rob much of the engine's power, so the driver must drive it in an emergency much differently than he would drive a factory SUV. In response to this need I developed a series of armored vehicle driving courses.

Around that time I was in my temporary living quarters (a beautiful beach house) in West Africa when I finished reading a fascinating book titled *Terror at Beslan: A Russian Tragedy with Lessons for America's Schools*, by Dr. John Giduck, in which he chronicles the story of the September 1, 2004 Beslan School Siege in Russia. The Beslan school hostage crisis, or Beslan massacre as it turned out, lasted three days, starting when a group of armed Islamic militants, mostly Ingush and Chechen, occupied School Number One in the town of Beslan, North Ossetia. Over 1,100 people were held as hostages, including 777 children, and it all ended in horror with the deaths of at least 334 people, including 186 children. It was a tragedy on an epic scale, and I struggled to read about how the authorities attempted to blow holes in walls and go to other extraordinary lengths to rescue the children and adults; all with little success. Dr. Giduck concluded in his book that America was very vulnerable to just such an attack, and that we had better prepare ourselves— because if we were unprepared, as Russia had been, we could very easily suffer the same tragic results. He also enumerated several groups in the U.S. who had been caught in the early stages of planning similar terror attacks.

The book was eye opening for me. To tell the truth, it made me realize how vulnerable we are. And that, as a parent, scared the hell out of me. Even with my international security background, I knew that if we were attacked in that same way—and heaven forbid, a multiple site coordinated attack—we did not have the best tools available to respond effectively. I didn't have the answer, but I knew that there must be something I could do to develop a system or tool to fight back if such an attack occurred. As soon as I returned from Africa I met with Shaun Bufton, a friend who served as the SWAT commander in my county, and I told him my concerns. In my own mind I was developing a system to fight back against a mass shooter, which is what I teach in Fight Back Nation and in this book. It is solid and effective. However, what do we do if terrorists take schools hostage? I told Shaun that I had concerns about the aftermath of a school shooting, and where wounded students couldn't be safely evacuated if the situation was drawn out. How could SWAT and medical teams get the wounded out if the area hadn't been secured? I had an idea, and it was something that could be utilized to not only evacuate wounded students, but also be deployed in the event of a hostage situation.

I merged the two things that were most on my mind lately—the need to go into the middle of hostile circumstances and my work with armored vehicles. I secured an investor and bought a Ford E-350 cargo van and began to develop an armored rescue vehicle based on Shaun's requirements. We developed an armored vehicle that holds a number of large and fully equipped men and is able to enter a school, college, mall, hospital or business building through the front door and travel through the hallways.

I call it the ASRV-FIST (Active Shooter Response Vehicle-First In Suppression Team), and it is the only fully armored rescue vehicle like it in the U.S. specifically built to go inside buildings during an active shooter event. It is outfitted with gun ports for shooting bad guys outside the van, and with lights that can be adjusted to be so bright a surgeon could work on a patient inside. It is armored so well that even if it ran over a grenade, it would just keep going. If students were trapped in a classroom, you can pull it up to the door, throw open the armored doors of the van, which have bullet-proof skirts that hang down, and children and teachers can jump into the van, and be transported to safety without any further danger. The back doors open and have protective ballistic skirts as well, so if the van pulls up to a classroom door and opens it's side doors and back doors, students can simply walk into the side doors and out of the back doors and walk down the hallway away from the shooters, protected by the van.

When the van was built and ready to debut at a law enforcement conference in St. George, Utah, I received a call from Dr. Giduck, the author who had inspired me to create a tool that law enforcement could use to combat hostage takers and school shooters. He told me that he had heard about the van, and that I had been inspired by his book to build it. He asked when I thought it would be ready to debut, because he would really like to see it at some point. I told him that I was putting it on the trailer to take to St. George for a Sheriff's Conference the following week, and it was ready to debut already.

"Really? You're kidding," he said. "I'm catching a plane for that conference next week. I'm the keynote speaker." He expressed that he was very interested and excited about the van.

It was unbelievable to me. Certainly, the stars had aligned for the inspiration of my armored van to be the keynote speaker at the conference where it was being introduced to law enforcement for the very first time. I couldn't believe the incredible odds of that call.

I returned to the trailer to get the van cinched down for the trip to St. George, and Shaun Bufton called me from the conference and asked, "Is the van loaded up yet?"

I chuckled to myself, because I assumed he was just excited for me to get the van to the conference. "Yeah, it's on the trailer and I'm getting it locked down for the trip down there."

"Well you better back it off," he said to my astonishment.

"What?"

"They need it in Alpine. Talk to Mike Smith. We've got a barricade situation, and they need the van."

Wow. The paint was still not quite dry and no one had seen it yet, and already the SWAT team had a definite need for it. I got the address and told him I would be there in under 20 minutes. I arrived on the scene and Mike asked what the van could do. I told him, "whatever you want it to do". He looked at me and said "Okay, see if you can deliver the team directly inside the garage."

I knew the van could do it, but I told him, "Look, Mike, I'm not active duty law enforcement any longer.

Mike looked at me like I had two heads. "So? You're the only one that knows what this van can do." Then he said something that sounded to me like, "you're deputized. Now get those guys in there!" Maybe I just heard what I wanted to, but regardless, he gave me the green light to deliver the team right into the garage of the target house. And there was nothing the suspect could do about it!

I dropped off the tactical team inside, then drove the sniper team up close to assess the situation, then picked up the bomb robot and delivered it inside the garage as well. We were able to do all of this because the bullet proof van allowed us to operate right on top of the "X" or ground zero of the incident. They told me that getting the robot inside before operating it saved a ton of battery use, making it much more effective.

The van showed up at the Sheriff's Conference and debuted with one real world mission under its belt. As of this writing the van has served over 400 successful missions. In one of those missions a bullet was fired directly at the driver and it glanced off the windshield just above the steering wheel leaving a small mark in the window. Other rounds penetrated the soft outer skin of the van but were stopped cold by the inner panels of ballistic steel. No officers were injured. It has saved many lives. The van is my gift to law enforcement in our region to ensure that they are better protected, and that our children and others have a better chance of surviving in the event of a hostage or terrorist situation. We are making this model of the van available to other law enforcement agencies. Dr. Giduck introduced me to Lt. Col. Dave Grossman, who is a world-renowned expert on homicide, and major fan and supporter of the van as well. When Dave Grossman was the keynote speaker at a local university he asked to come to the office and look the van over closely. He wrote in a letter:

> I am writing to thank you for the ASRV demo and to congratulate you on this excellent and innovative project.
>
> The ASRV is a revolutionary contribution to active shooter response, officer safety, personal security operations, and SWAT operations. I give my whole-hearted endorsement of the ASRV and your team who created it. It will save lives!

I'm hopeful that many law enforcement agencies are able to get the van for their jurisdictions, so they too can have the ability to enter a public space and level the playing field against a terrorist attack.

Chapter Eight — A Sad Day at Sutherland Springs

I landed at the airport in San Antonio, Texas on Sunday, November 5, 2017. I took my phone off of airplane mode and it quickly filled with several phone message and texts from my daughter Courtney. Courtney was a new police officer in Provo, Utah. I assumed she was okay, because she was the one trying to contact me—but the volume of messages told me that she was desperate to share some very serious news with me. I didn't take the time to read or listen, but I called her immediately.

"Dad, there's been a mass shooting at Sutherland Springs Baptist Church, not far from where you're going."

My business trip already routed me through Sutherland Springs. I instantly recalled the town. It was very small—an intersection with a blinking light in the middle of a flat Texas plain. I thanked her and looked up the news of the shooting on my phone as I headed for my rental car. Within 45 minutes I was in Sutherland Springs, and pulled in at the gas station where there were more police cars than residents. I saw people gathering water bottles from the convenience store and putting them in cars.

I went inside and saw a man and woman taking water

bottles out of the refrigerator, so I introduced myself and asked, "How can I help?"

The couple looked at me, the man's arms filled with bottles of water for the responding police officers and his eyes noticeably vacant. The woman spoke up and said, "I don't know. How *can* you help?"

I thought for a moment, then said, "I have some experience with critical incidents like this. I just want to know if there's something I can do for you guys."

"Yes," she responded quickly. "We don't know what to do. No one knows what to do. The mayor is over at the community center, and no one knows what to do. No one's tellin' us anything."

I could tell that she'd had some pent up frustration, and I certainly understood why. "Okay, I'm happy to help."

At that point the man raised his head a little and made eye contact with me. "I was the first one in the church." I could see the pain in his tired eyes. "I will never unsee what I saw today." He hesitated a moment, then said, "Tell me—tell me that there's a way. Tell me it goes away." The desperation in his face looked eternally chiseled in his features. I wasn't sure what I could possibly say to relieve his fear that he would live with that nightmare every moment for the rest of his life.

I finally said, "Look, it'll never go away. I've seen those things myself. But there'll come a time when it won't occupy every second of your thoughts." My heart went out to this poor man who had run in to a gruesome scene where many of his friends and neighbors had just been massacred as they worshipped God in the most defenseless place on earth. "I can tell you this—the more you help others, the less you will dwell on what you saw. Keep doing what you're doing."

Devin Patrick Kelley got out of his SUV around 11:20 a.m., wearing black tactical gear with a bulletproof vest and a black facemask with a white skull on the front. He grabbed his AR style semi-automatic rifle and a handful of loaded magazines. A Texas state law made it unlawful for him to purchase the rifle, but by definition, laws don't stop criminals and a computer glitch had missed his violent history in the background check. As he approached the occupied church he shot and killed two people. He then went inside and began to shoot worshipers sitting in the pews. He yelled, "Everybody dies, motherf@&#*rs," as he walked up and down the center aisle shooting, pausing to reload every 15 seconds or so.

Stephen Willeford had decided to stay home from church services that morning because he had to catch up on sleep for his upcoming shifts at the University Hospital where he was a plumber. In his mid 50s, Stephen was sometimes mistaken for Santa Claus by children at the store. He was jolted awake when his daughter Stephanie came into his bedroom and asked, "Do you hear gunfire?" He put his jeans on quickly and went to the living room where he could hear the distinct sound of gunshots. He rushed back to his bedroom and opened his gun safe and took out his AR-15 rifle and took only a moment to load a handful of rounds into a magazine. He hurried back to the living room and looked for his daughter, but saw her car pulling up in front of the house.

"I took a quick drive around the block, and there's a man wearing black tactical gear over at the Baptist church."

Stephen told her to get back inside, and gave her a job to keep her occupied: "Load another magazine for me." without taking time to put on his shoes, went running out of the house and up the street carrying his AR-15. As he approached the church, Stephan heard the shots ringing out from inside the church and he screamed as loud as he could,

"Hey!" Survivors inside the church report that the gunman heard the shout and immediately stopped shooting and headed for the front door. Stephan took cover behind a neighbor's truck and took aim over the hood, watching to see what happened next.

As Kelley exited the church in his black tactical gear he raised a pistol and fired off three shots at Stephen, who had taken a position of tactical advantage behind the truck. The truck was struck by gunfire as was another car behind Stephan.

Sutherland Springs Baptist Church

Stephen propped his AR-15 on the pickup's hood and put his holographic red dot site on the shooter's chest and fired twice. Kelley jerked, but didn't go down, indicating to Stephen that he was probably wearing a ballistic vest. The shooter immediately ran for a white SUV that was idling outside the church, about 60 feet from Stephen. As Kelley headed toward the white SUV Stephen noticed the black bullet proof vest didn't cover the sides of his torso, so he fired twice, striking him beneath the armpit and in the thigh. He knew the shot through the ribs had to be a serious wound. The shooter jumped into his SUV and fired off two more shots at Stephen through the window. Stephen returned fire aiming at the shooter's head; those shots shattering the window. The SUV took off and Stephen ran barefoot into the street firing another round into Kelley's rear window.

Stephen looked around and saw a blue pickup sitting in the intersection where 27-year-old Johnnie Langendorff was on the phone with 9-1-1 telling them about a shootout in the middle of the street. "That guy just shot up the church," Stephen yelled toward Johnnie. "We need to stop him." Johnnie didn't hesitate, but popped up the locks on the doors so the older shoeless man could hop onto the seat beside him.

They took off at top speed in the direction the shooter had gone, approaching 100 m.p.h. at times. All the while they were keeping the 9-1-1 operator updated with their location and strategizing what they would need to do when they encountered the shooter. Stephen kept it to himself that he was desperately low on ammo with just two rounds in his AR-15. They followed closely for a short distance until the SUV veered off the road and through a fence into a field.

They stopped without getting too close to the vehicle. Stephen exited and positioned himself behind the front tire and propped his AR-15 over the hood as he waited for the final confrontation with the shooter. After a minute of watching the white SUV intently, Stephen heard a police cruiser pull up on the road behind him, and over the loudspeaker he heard the officer's orders, "Driver, put down your weapon and come out with your hands up."

Stephen Milleford laid his rifle on the hood and turned toward the squad car with his hands up.

"Not you!" the officer shouted getting out of the car. "I need you to back me up!"

When other officers arrived they sent in a drone and found Kelley dead in the front seat of his white SUV. Stephen Milleford had stopped his rampage and saved lives that day.

———

I thanked the despondent couple and ran over to the tiny white building that served as the community center. The church was just a couple of hundred yards away. I walked through the crowd and could see that cars and pickup trucks from other communities were unloading bottles of water and food. I was moved at the humanity these people demonstrated. Someone must have overheard me in the convenience store because he took me by the arm and led me to a couple of community officials, introducing me as a person with some experience in mass shooter situations.

They asked me and asked what I thought was happening back in the church where the dead bodies were still warm. No one really knew how many were dead, how many were merely wounded or how many had gotten out alive. Most of the people in the parking lot had family in the church that day, and now they were desperate to know if their family members were all right or not.

At one point a buzz began to circulate and I could hear distinctly that it was coming in my direction. It quickly arrived. "He was shot by Stephen Milleford. Did you hear? Stephen Milleford shot him and then he chased him before he could go back in and shoot more. He killed him!" The crowd was quietly electrified with the news that one of their own had ended the massacre prematurely, saving many lives, and the fact that there was swift justice repaid to the murderer seemed to be a little comforting to those around me. They were just a little bit less "victims" in that moment, and it lifted their spirits along with their hopes.

There were 26 dead, and another 20 shot and badly wounded. It was a very bad day in Sutherland Springs. It would have been much worse, but Stephen Milleford decided to fight back, and saved many lives in the process.

Chapter Nine — Inside a Mass Shooting

WHY?

Most of us hear about an attack on innocent people and are compelled to ask ourselves *why?* On May 3, 1999, following the Columbine High School massacre, Newsweek magazine asked the question in large print on the cover. Why would someone, anyone, attack defenseless people, especially children, and inflict such death and mayhem? What are the social and psychological reasons behind it? How did the attacker get the weapons? Is there a way to prevent these atrocious mass killings? Pundits and politicians wrestle publically with these questions, especially as they try to exploit them for their own political gain; but as of the time of this writing, little has been done to deter most active shooters.

The victims are varied, and innocent—children in school, Jews worshiping in synagogues or Muslims worshipping in mosques, or Christians in church or school. Every category of person seems to have a natural enemy. Therefore, we all need to embrace the fight back mentality and be better prepared to survive an active shooter incident.

The one thing we know from looking at past attacks is that most mass shooters are looking for soft targets where they can kill as many defenseless people as possible in the shortest time possible, without interference. That's why I dedicate myself to transforming soft targets into hardened targets, starting with schools.

At the Point a Shot is Fired, the WHY? Doesn't Matter

We have discussed the methods of stopping an attacker already, and you can clearly see that it is well worth the risk and potential sacrifice that is often required to stop a shooter. I have demonstrated to you that there is Warrior DNA inside all of us, and moreover, that there is a Momma Bear inside most of those who dedicate themselves to caring for and teaching the children of others.

Through our training we learn to flip that switch and activate the Fight Back DNA that we possess. As we have seen, some of those who fight back have been wounded. Some have been killed. I believe a simple training session on the fundamentals of **The Inside Leverage Takeaway** can improve anyone's odds of not only surviving an attack, but actually disarming and stopping the shooter. Armed with that powerful tool, we see that a teacher's success in protecting herself and her students will be much greater than the average Joe who assails the shooter with a random object. By properly training teachers, staff and office workers how to fight back against an active shooter, we harden the target considerably, rendering it much less attractive in the first place.

To better understand the dynamics of an active shooter incident, I include details of some of the most well-known mass shootings in this chapter. As tough as this chapter is to read, the information may help you better understand how these incidents evolved as well as make you think about what you might do differently if you find yourself in a similar situation.

The following chapter recounts in some detail a few mass shootings you may be aware of. Though the written details here are not overly graphic, the content in this chapter is heavy. There is certainly value in this information, but it is not required reading for you to gain an understanding of how to survive a mass shooting. The following incidents are not listed in chronological order.

Columbine High School

Littleton, Colorado
April 20, 1999

Eric Harris and Dylan Klebold were seniors at Columbine High School, and for more than a year had planned, and even openly discussed on social media and in school projects their desire to kill and shoot students in their high school. Some of their references to the massacre were slightly veiled while others were overt. In videos and journals they left behind, both expressed their intent to kill as many students as possible with bombs, knives and guns. They knew that approximately 500 students would be in the cafeteria at lunchtime, so they prepared bombs to go off in the cafeteria, hoping they would be powerful enough to cause the ceiling to crash down and kill most of them. They planted bombs in other locations around the campus, including the parking lot. As the bombs went off they planned to shoot and stab as many fleeing students as they could before law enforcement arrived—at which point they would simply kill themselves.

Harris left videos and notes at home when he left that morning; one that said: "It will be a day that will be remembered forever." They wanted to be famous, forever, and in a video Harris said it was their intent to "kick-start a revolution."

They placed several bombs around the town and the

school, all to divert law enforcement away from the main shooting gallery inside the high school. They even parked their cars in the parking lot, wired with large bombs set to go off at a time they assumed the lot would be filled with students, teachers and responders—noon.

The shooters first placed themselves where they could shoot the fleeing survivors of the cafeteria explosions as they ran to the parking lot, but moved to the staircase on a hill at the west side of the school when the bombs failed to detonate as planned.

At 11:19 a.m., when their bombs failed to go off, the shooters began to shoot students outside on the grass. Police were called immediately.

The shooters then entered the school through the west entrance, moving along the main north hallway, throwing pipe bombs and shooting at anyone they encountered. The shooters entered the library and yelled, "Get up!" They fired randomly, killing and injuring students. They put down their ammunition-filled duffel bags and reloaded their weapons, but no one attacked them during the reload. Of the 56 library hostages, they killed 10 and wounded 12.

They left the library and returned to the cafeteria, where Klebold lit a Molotov cocktail and threw it at the propane bomb. They left after two minutes, and the Molotov cocktail finally ignited, starting a small explosion and fire—which was quickly extinguished by the fire sprinklers. The shooters then wandered through the halls, looking in classrooms and taunting students hiding for their lives, but they stopped shooting. They meandered back up to the emptied library at 12:00, which was the time their car bombs were set to explode. The bombs failed to go off. Bored, the two shooters simply killed themselves.

Harris and Klebold killed 12 students and one teacher that day, and wounded 24 others.

What we learn from Columbine: One of the most prominent issues that we saw at Columbine was that there was no effective response plan in place for an active shooter at the school. Students had no idea what to do and staff was not sure what the proper protocol was. Many students were shot while hiding unprotected under desks and tables. They were trapped and unable to resist.

The law enforcement response was immediate, and the officers bravely entered the school to rescue critically injured students. However, at the time, passing injured students and open spaces while moving directly to engage the shooter was not the standard procedure. So, it was more that 40 minutes before the shooters were located by local SWAT team members. Post columbine, law-enforcement across the nation has whittled down the response time to an active shooter at a school to between 5 and 3 minutes from the time of the 911 call. Simply amazing!

Virginia Tech

Virginia Polytechnic Institute and State University
Blacksburg, Virginia
April 16, 2007

Shooter Seung-Hui Cho was a South Korean undergraduate student at the university, and a permanent U.S. resident. We discussed some of the main aspects of this event above, so we won't go through the details again here. During the two attacks, Cho killed five faculty members and 27 students, and wounded 17 others who survived. Six more were injured when they jumped from second-story windows to escape. To date, this is the worst school shooting on a US campus.

What we learn from Virginia Tech: Cho was a very small, weak, shy student armed with handguns and a simple chain and locks. He forced his way into classrooms where much larger students were on the other side of the door trying to hold it in place. He was successful because he fired rounds through the doors striking students on the other side. Using your body as a barricade against the door puts you in a very vulnerable position. In room 205 they successfully barricaded the door by placing a table against it, and then having two male students lay on the floor holding the table legs in place, effectively creating a human doorstop using the table and their bodies. Because they were laying on the floor supporting the table, when Cho fired through the door his rounds were well above the students and did not strike anybody. Room 205 is one of the only rooms that suffered no casualties during this mass shooting. Imagine if every classroom in Norris Hall had the ability to be locked from the inside of the room. Different outcome.

If we do not have a plan and are not willing to physically fight back against an active shooter, even a small, weak, untrained attacker can inflict significant casualties.

New Zealand Christchurch Mosques
Christchurch, New Zealand
March 15, 2019

Brenton Tarrant is a 28-year-old man from Grafton, New South Wales, Australia. He was very angry about so many Muslims relocating to Australia and New Zealand. He was active in global political movements to resist the prolifera-tion of Islamism and Islamic terrorism throughout Europe, the Middle East and the South Pacific. For two years he methodically planned his attacks in New Zealand, including the weapons he would use, how he would reload on the move, how to broadcast the attack live-stream and the locations of both mass shootings and his routes between the two. Although New Zealand has very strict gun laws, Tarrant was able to legally purchase several firearms, and possessed five guns at the scene: two semi-automatic AR style rifles, two shotguns and a lever-action firearm.

Al Noor Mosque. The Al Noor Mosque, Riccarton, generally had between 300 and 500 attendees at Friday afternoon prayer. Tarrant arrived and opened fire on patrons at 1:40 p.m., starting with the door greeter. He killed three more as he entered, walking with the rifle held at the tactical ready position (elevated to eye level) as he shot anyone he encountered. Naeem Rashid charged at the shooter from the front and was shot, and later died from his injuries. A neighbor saw Tarrant flee and drop a firearm in the driveway. Back outside, Tarrant shot more people, then went to his vehicle and retrieved another weapon from his trunk before returning to the mosque and again opening fire. No one attacked him as he went for additional weapons and ammunition in his trunk. He went back inside and continued his rampage for a couple of minutes before fleeing the mosque He had spent a total of six minutes at the scene by the time he left, heading towards his second target.

Linwood Islamic Centre. The second attack began at about 1:55 p.m. at the Linwood Islamic Centre, just 15 minutes after the first attack had begun. Tarrant appeared to be confused because he was unable to find the mosque's main door, so he started shooting people outside the mosque and through a window.

Inside, Abdul Aziz, a 48-year-old Afghan refugee, was praying with his family and about 80 other people when he heard gunshots. Aziz knew what he heard and immediately made the decision to confront the gunman in an attempt to buy time for the others to escape or hide. Aziz grabbed the first thing he could find to use as a weapon, which happened to be a handheld credit card machine, and raced outside to try to distract the shooter.

At this point Tarrant had discarded a shotgun, which was empty, and had run to his car to grab another weapon. Without hesitating, Aziz picked up the discarded weapon and tried to fire it, only to realize that there was no ammunition in the gun.

"I was screaming to the guy, 'Come I'm here, come I'm here.' I tried to put his focus on me. I didn't want him to go inside the mosque," Aziz related in an interview with Sky News. Aziz saw the hesitation and temporary confusion his actions were causing the shooter. He charged forward and hurled the shotgun at the shooters vehicle, smashing out the back window as the gunman fled the scene. Aziz's actions saved many lives that day.

Prime Minister Jacinda Ardern soon revealed that Tarrant had been planning to continue the attacks at a third location; either the mosque in Ashburton or the An-Nur Child Care Centre in Hornby. He explained, "There were two other firearms in the vehicle that the offender was in and it absolutely was his intention to continue with his attack." Police Commissioner Mike Bush corroborated this.

Fifty-one people, 47 male and 4 female, were killed in the attacks: 42 at the Al Noor Mosque, and 7 at the Linwood Islamic Centre. I am convinced that the number was anticipated to be much higher—but was not because of the heroic act of Abdul Aziz, who interfered with the shooter, causing him to go into Condition Black, and flee the scene and be subsequently apprehended by police.

What we learn from New Zealand: Abdul Aziz Wahabzada ended the attack prematurely by interfering with the shooter as he went outside for more ammunition. Throwing the shotgun at his car and breaking the windshield startled him to the point he decided to leave the scene, and it appears that many dozens of lives were likely spared by that effort. A shooter is most vulnerable as he attempts to reload his weapon. If you are in close proximity, this is the best time to attack the shooter.

Pulse Nightclub

Orlando, Florida

June 12, 2016

Omar Mateen, a 29-year-old Arab-American security guard with radical Islamic beliefs targeted the crowded Pulse nightclub in Orlando. Mateen, now a radicalized Islamic Extremist, considered himself a member of ISIS. As such, he believed gay men to be in serious defiance of Islamic Sharia Law and felt that because they were Americans, their justifiable deaths would send a message about our nation's activities in Islamic countries in the Middle East and elsewhere. He wanted this to be an ISIS terrorist attack with a political message, so he was prepared to engage police in an extended gunfight.

About 320 people were inside the club that Saturday night, now 2:00 a.m. Sunday morning as last call was announced. Mateen approached the entrance armed with a semi-automatic handgun and a semi-automatic AR style rifle. He also carried a bomb. Orlando Police (OPD) Officer Adam Gruler, was working extra duty in full uniform as security at the club entrance when he heard gunshots and rushed in and engaged Mateen. Mateen had already killed and injured numerous patrons as they danced on the dark night club floor. There was an intense exchange of gunfire and he felt outgunned and retreated, calling for backup. Two additional OPD officers arrived within two minutes. Gruler shouted "He's in the patio!" and resumed firing at Mateen. Mateen retreated deeper into the nightclub and barricaded behind his hostages.

Many patrons heard Mateen claim he had explosives as well as snipers stationed around the club, so they reported these two details in their 9-1-1 calls, probably delaying a law enforcement assault on Mateen. Many of the dancers had assumed the gunshots were fireworks or part of the music at first, and failed to take cover or run away. Many were killed on the dance floor, and many others were cowering in corners and huddled against walls, not knowing how to defend themselves. A recently discharged Marine veteran working as a bouncer had immediately recognized the sound of gunfire, and made his way through a locked door where he found 70 people hiding and paralyzed with fear. He quickly opened a latched door behind them helping them to escape. Meanwhile, Mateen roamed freely through the back of the club, shooting patrons at will. At some point, he made his way into the bathrooms. Patrons were huddled inside, with nowhere to go. No escape. He eventually killed numerous trapped people in both bathrooms. Mateen made multiple calls to 9-1-1 to make political statements about his Islamic cause. Within 15 minutes of the first shots, the police response seems to shift from an active shooter to that of a hostage scenario.

At 5:07 a.m., three hours after the first shot was fired, a policeman drove a BearCat armored vehicle through a wall in the northern bathroom and 14 SWAT officers successfully breached the building and killed Mateen. Omar Mateen killed 49 people and wounded at least 53.

What we learn from Pulse: The patrons were primarily able bodied men. In the dimly lit club, they should have had an opportunity to mount a counter attack. Many patrons fled to the bathrooms where there was only one way in and one way out. They were trapped. Again, there could have been opportunities to attack the shooter as he came into the bathroom. These observations are not a reflection of inaction for lack of courage, but rather an example of things that are in our favor that are often overlooked under stressful circumstances. And make no mistake about it, there were numerous selfless acts of heroism that night at the Pulse Night Club.

Sandy Hook Elementary School
Newtown, Connecticut
December 14, 2012

Adam Lanza had a history of anxiety and uneasiness in social situations. On the morning of December 14, the 20-year old went into his mother's room as she slept and shot her with one of her own guns.

Nearby Sandy Hook Elementary School, where Adam had attended as a child, had 456 children enrolled in kindergarten through fourth grade, and had recently undergone several top-notch security upgrades. After murdering his mother, Adam Lanza drove her car to the local grade school. The school's new security protocols required visitors to be individually admitted after visual and identification review by video monitor. The school's doors were locked at 9:30 a.m. each day, after morning arrivals. At 9:35 he arrived at the school and used his mother's semi-automatic AR style rifle to shoot out the glass panel next to the locked front doors. Morning announcements were being broadcast throughout the school, so as Lanza started shooting, most of the classes could hear the shots in the background of the intercom system.

Principal Dawn Hochsprung and school psychologist Mary Sherlach were meeting with other faculty members when they heard loud popping noises. They and lead teacher Natalie Hammond went out into the hall to see what was happening, and encountered Lanza. They called out

"Shooter! Stay put!" The shooter turned in their direction and opened fire. Hammond was hit twice, and crawled to the conference room and pressed her body against the door to keep it closed. Lanza entered the main office but didn't see the people hiding inside and went back to the hallway. School nurse Sarah (Sally) Cox hid under a desk in her office and could see Lanza's feet facing her from across the room, but he didn't see her, and left. She and the school secretary Barbara Halstead called 9-1-1 and hid in a first-aid supply closet, remaining there for the next four hours. Janitor Rick Thorne ran through hallways, alerting classrooms of the active shooter.

First grade teacher Kaitlin Roig hid 14 students in the class bathroom and barricaded the door, telling them to be completely quiet to remain safe. Lanza passed her classroom because it looked empty. School library staff Yvonne Cech and Maryann Jacob hid 18 children in a part of the library used for lockdown drills, but because the door wouldn't lock, they had the children crawl into a storage room, where Cech barricaded the door with a filing cabinet. None of them was injured. Music teacher Maryrose Kristopik barricaded her fourth-graders in a tiny supply closet and when Lanza arrived moments later and pounded on the door and yelled, "Let me in," they remained quiet and he moved on. I will not go into detail about what happened in the following minutes. Suffice it to say heartbreaking and tragic is a gross understatement.

At 9:40 Lanza pulled out one of the two semi-automatic pistols he had brought with him, and shot himself in the head. The rampage lasted only 5 minutes.

Twenty students, eight boys and twelve girls, all either six or seven years old, were dead. All six dead adults were women who worked at the school. Two more students were wounded.

What we learn from Sandy Hook: Although the school had invested heavily in physical security upgrades, the shooter simply shot out a window and walked in. We know of safety film that schools can adhere to glass, that when shot holds the glass together so shooters can't simply walk through. Whatever a school chooses to do to harden the buildings, training the teachers and staff how to properly run, hide, or fight if confronted by an active shooter needs to be a priority. Teachers must be taught to turn off the lights, lock the door and place an adequate barricade in front of it; then if the shooter forces his way in through all of that, plan to attack him as he comes through the doorway. In those rooms where the teachers were able to lock and barricade the doors, the children were safe. He did not spend time trying to gain entry into classrooms that were locked or seemed empty.

Below are some additional mass shooting events in America—a partial list only. As I considered which events to share in these pages, taking into consideration what I felt would be most instructive for the reader, I felt the ones above were best to illustrate the experience, if you ever find yourself in the middle of an attack. Being present during a mass shooting is a worst case scenario most of us will never experience. However, for those few who will, you need to know what to expect, and how to mitigate the damage. That's why we review these real-life shootings. It's life or death, and if you don't successfully Run or Hide, you absolutely must Fight Back.

Killeen, Texas, October 16, 1991 — 23 dead, 27 wounded

Fort Hood, Texas, November 5, 2009 — 13 dead, 30 wounded

San Bernardino Shooting, California, December 2, 2015 — 14 dead, 22 wounded

Marjory Stoneman Douglas High School, Parkland, Florida, February 14, 2018 — 17 dead, 17 wounded

Santa Fe High School, Texas, May 18, 2018 — 10 dead, 13 injured

Tree of Life Synagogue, Pittsburgh, October 27, 2018 – 11 dead, 6 wounded

Thousand Oaks, California, November 7, 2018 — 13 dead, 18 injured

Virginia Beach, Virginia, May 31, 2019 — 12 dead, 5 wounded

El Paso Walmart, Texas, August 3, 2019 — 22 dead, 24 wounded

Dayton, Ohio, August 4, 2019 – 9 dead, 27 wounded

Unfortunately, several mass shootings occurred during the writing of this book. It is difficult to keep up with the ghastly phenomenon. In the next chapter we review several mass shooting events where people chose to fight back and launched a counter-attack that resulted in saving lives.

Chapter Ten — Interrupting a Mass Shooting

There are several active shooter and mass shooter incidents that most of us have never heard about. This is because they were stopped or severely limited by someone fighting back and preventing the kind of carnage that we read about in the cases where almost no one chose to fight back. Fighting back doesn't guarantee that no one gets hurt. In every case I've ever heard of, however, where someone decided to fight back, the numbers of those wounded or killed by the shooter were severely limited by that action. In fact, in almost every case, the shooter's rampage was stopped, and he was either disarmed or killed. Following are some examples.

Parkrose High School

Portland, Oregon
May 17, 2019

Angel Granados-Diaz, an 18-year-old Parkrose High School student in Portland, Oregon, was visibly distraught as he entered a classroom right before lunch wearing a black trench coat under which he hid a shotgun. He had stopped in various classrooms asking the whereabouts of specific students, frustrated when he didn't get his answer. He finally grew tired of looking for specific targets and pulled the shotgun from beneath his trench coat, causing students to scatter and hide. He had carried a shotgun into the school with the intent of shooting as many helpless students as possible before being shot and killed by police himself.

Security guard Keanon Lowe would have none of it. He immediately saw the danger and rushed Granados-Diaz, and tackled him football style, and wrestled the shotgun out of his hands. It was over at that point. Granados-Diaz was done.

Keanon Lowe had been a prominent high school and college football player in Oregon, and was now a coach at Parkrose High School. His day job at the school was security guard, and he took his job seriously. Thanks to his courage and willingness to engage the shooter, not a shot was fired that day, so of course, not a single student was wounded or killed. Thanks to his valor and decisive action, many innocent lives were saved that day.

Waffle House
Nashville, Tennessee
April 22, 2018

Late in the evening of Saturday, April 22, Travis Reinking exited his truck in the parking lot of the Antioch Waffle House in Tennessee armed with an AR15 rifle. As he approached the restaurant he fatally shot two people near the entrance. He then entered the Waffle House and fired on people inside, instantly killing a third person and fatally wounding a fourth. Other patrons scrambled, diving for cover in an attempt to escape the gunfire.

James Shaw Jr., a 29-year old African-American man with a young daughter at home, landed on the floor near the bathroom as a bullet grazed his elbow. He scrambled to get just inside the door, but quickly realized there were only two directions for him to go—into the restroom, which he knew only had the single entrance and exit, or toward the shooter.

"In the bathroom, it's only one way in and one way out, and I was like, he's going to have to work for this kill — for me, personally." Shaw said.

There was a pause in the shooting and he assumed the shooter was reloading or fixing a malfunction. Shaw made a snap decision that it was better to fight back than to wait to be shot. He sprang into action and lunged at the shooter.

"I just got a head full of steam, and I ran through the door. And it worked out like I wanted it to." In spite of the hot rifle barrel burning his hand, Shaw ripped the gun away from the shooter, stopping the murderous rampage. The killing stopped.

Shaw says that the shooter was very surprised that Shaw attacked him, and was talking to him as they wrestled, telling him he was messing everything up. The shooter ran away naked only to be taken into custody by police the next day.

Metro Nashville Police spokesperson Don Aaron said of James Shaw Jr., "He is the hero here, and no doubt he saved many lives."

He was smart, and realized that the only way for him and others to survive was to simply attack the shooter and fight back. Fighting back was the answer.

Noblesville West Middle School

Noblesville, Indiana

May 25, 2018

The 7th grade 13-year old shooter, unnamed, had been performing Internet searches like, "Columbine," "Sandy Hook," "school shooting memes," "what was the largest mass shooting in America," and "Noblesville West Middle School blueprint." His family had guns in the safe downstairs, and he had been instructed in gun safety.

The day before the shooting, the 7th grader filmed a two-minute video in his family's basement showing a .45-caliber handgun and a .22 caliber handgun with a silencer attached. He said on the video, "Tomorrow's Friday; you know what that means. I have to take other people's lives before I take my own." That evening he warned three classmates with text messages that read: "Don't come to school tomorrow."

The shooter's mother said that the morning of the shooting was normal, and he got ready for school and talked about an upcoming band concert. He then left for school with the weapons in his backpack, and put the bag in his locker and went to class. During his second period science class with Jason Seaman, students took a quiz on school-issued iPads. The shooter finished early and asked to be excused. He went to his locker, got his backpack and headed to the bathroom, where he left the bag.

Mr. Seaman was holding a small basketball in his hand and helping student Ella Whistler with a question about the quiz when he heard a knock on the classroom door. He motioned for another student to open the door. The shooter walked into the classroom with his weapons hidden in his hooded sweatshirt. As he walked in he immediately pulled out the .22 and shot Mr. Seaman. Mr. Seaman reacted by throwing the basketball at the shooter as hard as he could and simultaneously rushed him. Before he could react Mr. Seaman had him in a tight bear hug. The shooter kept firing at the teacher, striking him and Ella Whistler numerous times. Mr. Seaman held the shooter and pinned him to the ground, which caused him to drop the weapon. Mr. Seaman shouted for other students to "Run, get out of the classroom, and call 9-1-1."

Despite being shot, Jason Seaman chose to fight back without hesitation and his quick and courageous actions saved lives that day.

Tallahassee Yoga Studio
Tallahassee, Florida
November 2, 2018

Scott Beierle was a schoolteacher, and had moved around and changed jobs a great deal due to problems related to groping and insulting women. He appears to have been a racist and misogynist. He purchased a pistol in July and for months planned his assault on the Tallahassee Hot Yoga studio. Before going to the class he stopped at the store and purchased a yoga mat and earplugs. This would be his first and last yoga class.

Beierle arrived early for the class, and walked around impatiently outside, then entered the studio at 5:37 p.m. as it began. Without warning he pulled the pistol from his bag and shot two women in the class from behind; college student Maura Binkley, 21, and Dr. Nancy Van Vessem, 61. Everyone scrambled to escape the shooter as he continued to fire randomly at the women.

Joshua Quick was a student in the class, and had initially huddled against the wall with the women—but when he perceived that there was a pause in the shooting, he quickly realized that they would all be killed if they failed to fight back. Joshua glanced around for something to use as a weapon, and the only thing he could get to quickly was a vacuum cleaner against the wall. He lunged for the vacuum and grabbed it.

He tells the story: "We were huddled in a corner . . . and as he made his way over toward us, he stopped firing. I don't know if it jammed or what was going on. I picked up the only thing nearby to hit him with, which was a vacuum cleaner, and I hit him over the head."

The shooter reacted by striking Joshua in the head and face with his handgun.

"I felt myself fall to the ground. I didn't lose consciousness. I jumped up, ran over and grabbed the only other thing that I could find — which is a broomstick — and I hit him over the head with that. Again, he pushed me off, but some people were able to run out of the room."

The shooter was suddenly confused, and stopped trying to shoot those in the room. He simply turned the gun on himself and fired, killing himself.

Tallahassee Police Chief Michael DeLeo said Joshua Quick, "fought back and tried not only to save himself but other people." His actions, he said, were "a testament to the courage of the people who don't just turn and run, but the strength of our community and the spirit of those people trying to help and save and protect others."

Joshua Quick's fast thinking and courageous actions saved many lives that day.

University of North Carolina at Charlotte
Charlotte, North Carolina
April 30, 2019

April 30 at 5:50 p.m. Trystan Terrell entered the Kennedy Building on the campus, heading for Room 236, his former classroom. He was dressed in black and entered the large room where 60 classmates were delivering their final group presentations. He smiled, then began to shoot students randomly as they scattered and ducked for cover.

Riley Howell was a student in the class, and was tall and

athletic. As bullets filled the room and four students went down, Riley didn't hesitate, but lunged for and tackled Terrell. Riley took three bullets before Terrell stopped shooting, the third killing him. Riley was the last person shot that day. His willingness to fight back stopped Terrell from shooting anyone else and taking any more lives. One other student died, and three survived their wounds.

Charlotte-Mecklenburg Police Chief Kerr Putney praised Howell in a news conference, saying, "He took the fight to the assailant . . . he saved lives doing so. What he did was he took the assailant off his feet, and then the heroes we have here [police officers] were able to apprehend him."

Again, the shooter intended to kill dozens of helpless students that day. The moment that Riley Howell decided to fight back, the rampage was over. Riley Howell gave his life, rather than let Terrell take it from him. His actions saved classmates in that room and possibly others around the campus that day.

STEM School in Highlands Ranch
Highland Ranch, Colorado
May 7, 2019

On May 7 Devon Erickson entered the STEM School in Highlands Ranch, Colorado and pulled out a gun and yelled, "Nobody move." Kendrick Castillo saw that Erickson was about to start shooting, and without hesitating Kendrick jumped on Erickson and wrestled him for the gun. During the fight, Erickson fired the gun, fatally striking Kendrick in the chest. His attack on the shooter gave fellow students Joshua Jones and Brendan Bialy the opportunity they needed to subdue Erickson. Joshua was shot in the leg and hip but was able to take the gun away before any other students were killed. He kept Erickson pinned until the police arrived moments later.

Again, because of the brave actions of these three young students, Devon Erickson was not allowed to wander through the school shooting helpless victims at will. Kendrick Castillo, Joshua Jones and Brendan Bialy had two choices—wait to be shot, or fight back. By choosing to fight back they minimized the damage Erickson was able to inflict on their fellow students that day.

Seattle Pacific University
Seattle, Washington
June 5, 2014

In the days prior to June 4, 27-year-old Aaron Ybarra of Mountlake Terrace visited the Christian SPU campus and convinced two of its female students to give him a private tour of the school. As they escorted him through Otto Miller Hall, Ybarra looked for possible escape routes. At 3:00 p.m. on June 4, Ybarra drove by Otto Miller Hall to ensure it was packed with students at that time of day. The next day Ybarra walked onto the campus with a shotgun and extra ammunition, and a large hunting knife.

Ybarra walked up to Paul Lee and showed him the gun. Lee didn't seem scared by the rifle. So Ybarra shot him in the back of the head. Pellets from the blast also hit Thomas Fowler who was standing a few feet away. Ybarra tried to immediately fire on a female student nearby but his gun misfired and she had time to run away. He reloaded and continued inside Otto Miller Hall where he found student Tristian Cooper-Roth seated at a table. He told Cooper-Roth, "I just shot a man outside for disrespecting me. Now don't move." Ybarra then saw student Sarah Williams walking down the stairs of Otto Miller Hall and he shot her in the upper torso. Cooper-Roth started to run and Ybarra swung the shotgun around to shoot him, but his gun misfired again.

Jon Meis was a student-safety monitor on duty at SPU that day. He heard someone shout, "Nobody move!" and looked to see where several students stood frozen with their hands in the air. He wasn't sure what was going on, or what he could do to stop it. He was unarmed—with the exception of some pepper spray he carried. A shot rang out causing everyone to jump, and the captive students ran in all directions.

Jon could see that Ybarra had opened his shotgun and was reloading it, and decided that was the moment to attack him. With only pepper spray in hand, he rushed the shooter and sprayed him in the face and head and immediately followed that up by grabbing the rifle and wrestling the shooter to the floor. Ybarra resisted, but Jon was surprised how easy it was to take the rifle from the shooter. Jon ran back to the security room and shoved the rifle inside. When he looked back he saw that Ybarra started to reach into what appeared to be his waistband or a large pocket. Jon thought he was going for a handgun and would start shooting again. He rushed back over to him and grabbed him from behind, causing the large hunting knife to bounce to the floor along with a couple dozen shotgun rounds. Ybarra told Jon, "You shouldn't have taken my knife away from me. I was gonna cut my throat."

Police arrived within minutes, and took Ybarra into custody. When interviewed by police the shooter said he was surprised when Jon Meis attacked him. It wasn't what he was expecting. Without a doubt, Jon's decisive actions saved lives that day.

Marysville-Pilchuck High School
Marysville, Washington
October 24, 2014

Jaylen Fryberg, a 15-year-old student at Marysville-Pilchuck High School was a member of a prominent family from the Tulalip Indian tribes and a very popular freshman on the high school football team.

Fryberg wanted to date a particular girl at the school, who was dating his cousin. She told him she wasn't available. On Friday, October 24, Fryberg sent texts inviting several students, all of whom were close friends and relatives, to meet him for lunch at a certain table, even urging some to skip classes to be together. Minutes prior to the shooting Fryberg sent a group text to his family and the families of his would-be victims, stating, "I need to do this," and apologizing for his actions, and laying out plans for his own funeral.

Fryberg entered the school cafeteria and sat down at a different table, then at 10:39 a.m. he stood up, approached the table where his friends and relatives were sitting, and pulled out a .40 caliber handgun and fired at least eight shots, methodically shooting some of the students in the head.

Students ran outside frantically while others ran and huddled inside classrooms as Fryberg started to shoot randomly around the campus.

First-year social studies teacher Megan Silberberger was in an office next door to the cafeteria when she heard gunfire and ran into the cafeteria. She saw the students on the ground and saw the shooter, and ran toward the shooter and confronted him, saying, 'Stop, stop, stop!'

Some report that she grabbed Fryberg's arm—the one with the gun in his hand. No one is sure if the action caused the next round to accidentally discharge and hit Fryberg in his own neck, or if he realized it was over at that point and purposefully pointed the gun at himself and pulled the trigger; but within a second it was over.

Tragically, one student was killed and four others were

injured in the shooting.

Megan Silberberger said, "I reacted exactly like all my colleagues would in this type of event. I am a schoolteacher, and like all teachers, I am committed to the safety and well-being of my students." Her quick thinking and immediate action stopped the shooter from injuring or killing anyone else.

New England Pentecostal Ministries
Pelham, New Hampshire
October 12, 2019

As we were editing this book for publication a would-be church mass shooting came across the networks from Pelham, New Hampshire. Dale Holloway, a 37-year-old man barged into the church during a wedding ceremony and rushed up to the front and shot the minister, 75-year-old Stanley Choate, in the chest.

Angelo Castiglione, the groom's father describes what happened. "I saw a figure in black just run right up the stairs and face the bishop. The bishop turned around. Just 'boom, boom' and then he [the shooter] turned around and aimed at my son and his future wife." At that point he shot the bride, 60-year-old Claire McMullen, in the arm, and turned to fire on others.

The groom, 60-year-old Mark Castiglione, lunged at the shooter and wrestled the gun away from him before he could shoot anyone else. Although he was struck in the head with the gun during the struggle, no one else was shot. Other wedding guests likewise counter-attacked the shooter, ending his rampage. It was over before anyone was killed.

Thanks to the quick counter-attack by the groom, no one was killed that Saturday afternoon.

In almost every instance where a person counter attacks the shooter, lives are saved. Sometimes the one who disrupts the shooter loses his or her life. However, not fighting back or launching a counter-attack would likely result in being shot anyway. These are just a few examples of successful outcomes when people react without hesitation and choose to Fight Back.

Chapter Eleven — Schools Are Fighting Back

Many schools are implementing our Fight Back Nation program. Below are the feelings of two administrators who are responsible for hundreds of teachers and staff and many thousands of students. They share their Fight Back journey with us, to help us understand the evolution of making schools hard targets, and eliminating the fear and feelings of victimhood from their numbers.

Dr. Rick L. Robins, Ed.D.

Superintendent, Juab School District
Nephi, Utah

Like all school districts we are extremely interested in protecting the students in our schools, and we run the mandatory drills and alarms and provide all of the training to ensure their safety. All of this we do with the expectation that nothing will ever happen. Yet, in the back of your mind you wonder what will happen and what will our people do if anything like this ever occurs. It's really unfortunate that we live in an age where every teacher, every parent and every student think about that—what happens if it occurs at my school? In reality, we live with the truth that this really can occur, and no one is immune from the threat.

With that in mind, we didn't have a particular response plan in place, but were very concerned about what we should do to prepare for the possibility of an active shooter on the school grounds. One evening I received a call from our School Board President who told me she happened to be invited to a training being provided to another school district by Fight Back Nation, and I was really surprised at how excited and enthusiastic she was about the training. She praised the training and the simple, common sense methodologies Fight Back Nation provides, and told me she was convinced that the system they teach is completely compatible with what our district was looking for. We had already made the determination that standing still and being victims was not the strategy we were going to pursue. We just didn't know what could be done to resist or even thwart a school shooter. As she explained her training to me, I thought it made perfect sense, and was completely intuitive. I got Dave's contact information and called him, and after learning more about the training program, I presented it to the school board and we decided to have Fight Back Nation come in and train our entire school district.

Our district had already established three key elements relating to the school shooter problem in our nation. Our three-prong plan consisted of the following.

The first prong of our plan is recognition that we have a mental health crisis. This is undeniable. There are a lot of disturbed people in our society, and whether they are students at our schools or unhinged people living within our local communities, we would like to find a way to reach them and help them before they reach the boiling over point. Statistically speaking, most school shooters come from within the student population, so providing "whole child" mental health services throughout the district is the first element of our strategic plan.

The second element is physical infrastructure. We knew we needed to reinforce our security layers, like a single point entry, bulletproofing glass, and installing camera surveillance systems and other technologies.

Fight Back Nation showed us how to better partner with our local law enforcement agencies to coordinate our efforts. We now invite them to perform drills at our schools, especially on weekends, and provide them with free breakfast and lunch in the cafeteria with our students any time they feel like dropping in. They have become part of the daily culture of our schools. We also went the extra step and provided local police departments with office space in our school buildings, where detectives do much of their paperwork. Their frequent presence provides the schools with an added layer of 'hardening' in the eyes of the public—especially would-be attackers.

The third element is training. Through Fight Back Nation we provide the correct training, including knowledge and skills, to our teachers and staff. With Dave's help we 'empower' our teachers and staff to be 'that person' if they find themselves the one to confront an attacker. Male or female—size, strength and age don't matter—every one of our staff can execute the techniques taught to us by Fight Back Nation, and can confront an assailant. Following the first training we received I had several teachers and staff members come to me to share:

> "These have been the best professional development activities I've ever been involved in. I'm so confident now, about myself and what I can do in the classroom to protect myself and my students, that all of the uneasiness I've been

feeling for so long has been changed. I just feel so confident now if anything ever happens."

The added bonus to this feeling of confidence and empowerment experienced by our teachers and staff after their training is that it extends into every area of their life. They approach their job and their lives without the foreboding fear that they used to have all the time. The level of relief and confidence of our school district employees makes it impossible for me to even put a value on the training we've received. Our average young, female teacher, who often weighs no more than 110 pounds, is now filled with confidence—in and out of the classroom.

The teachers and staff have really opened up around the campuses, and are having candid and open conversations about security and everything else that benefits our students and school environment. All of the energy that used to be wasted on fear is being repurposed, and I see barriers coming down, and energy going into their careers and personal lives. Not many of them complain about being pushed around in any aspect of their personal or professional lives any longer. They have been truly transformed through this empowerment. To put it simply—they are no longer victims.

The response from parents in our district has been similar. All of the responses have been 100 percent positive. "Thank you for keeping my child safe." I hear it so often. Parents in other school districts email me asking if I can help get the Fight Back nation training in their school district, asking me to please speak with their superintendent and school board.

My Aha! Moment—The realization that the shooter at Virginia Tech went and reloaded while strong young college men remained huddled against a wall in a classroom waiting for him to return and kill them, while passengers on any airplane will pile on and attack any person making the slightest threat—it very much illustrated to me that we can no longer sit around being sheep, waiting to be slaughtered. No wonder our teachers were constantly filled with anxiety. No more. It is no longer like that in our school district. Our teachers and staff now recognize that their momma bear instinct plus the skills they've learned give them a real fighting chance in the event of an attack. There are no victims in our schools. There are only professionals who are prepared to do what it takes if a crazy attacker happens to be foolish enough to select one of our schools. If a shooter comes to one of our schools, it won't be an easy target for him, and he will pay a price for it.

Following the training we received from Fight Back Nation, we had an incident that really helped illustrate the value of their training. A woman high on meth exited the freeway and came screaming into the parking lot of one of our schools. I just happened to be visiting at that particular school at the time, so I watched it all in real-time with the school board member who was with me. The drugged woman got out of her car and started to go around the school yelling and banging hard on the glass of every door, demanding that they let her in. Of course, the school went immediately into lockdown mode. We simply can't know the intent of such a person, or if she has a gun, or a knife, or a bomb, or if she is looking for someone in particular. We joined the principal and watched the woman on the live camera monitor system. It was extremely impressive to see our teachers respond so quickly, every one of them thinking clearly and doing exactly what they were trained to do. Within mere seconds the campus was a ghost town—not a single student was left unattended in a hallway or restroom. Our messaging system sent instant notices to all of the parents of the students letting them know what was happening, and asking them to stay away for a few minutes as police handled the matter.

In fact, the police were able to find the woman after she fled the site and they took her in. As we watched the scene unfold live and witnessed the confidence and clearheaded actions of every teacher, I knew that everything we had done to protect against an attack had been correct. There were no victims—no posttraumatic stress at the thought of an attack. All of our teachers and staff were cheery and confident. The thing we did learn that day was that we needed to improve our parent-student unification system after such an event. Dave helped us with that too.

Even the students seemed completely stress free following the incident. Something that Fight Back Nation teaches our teachers and staff in the training is to be aware of the feelings of fear in the students during a lockdown—or especially if they think there might be an active shooter on the campus. Dave teaches the teachers to engage the students, and give them something to do, to let them know things are good. The teachers explains to the students what she is doing, and why. She says,

> "Okay, first I'm locking the door. I do it because no active shooter has ever come through a locked door in a school. But, help me put my desk against the door in case he decides to be the first. Then I turn off the lights. The lights are bright in the hallway, so if he comes in here, it will take a few seconds for his eyes to adjust to our lower light. If a bad guy did happen to come through our locked door, I have been trained to fight back. If he comes through the door, as his eyes are adjusting to are dark room, I will attack him! I want some of

you to watch the window, because at the point police officers are on the school grounds, they will go immediately to the bad guy and stop him. So let me know when you see police officers."

Each of these things the teacher says to her students helps them understand what to expect and that the teacher and the school are very well prepared for this. They are watching for the police to arrive—at which point they know everything is fine. The important part: they are not sitting around shaking with the belief that they are going to be shot and killed at any second.

I received a report from some of the students that during the beginning of the incident, about 50 of them were alone in the gym area, which doubles as a lunchroom. As soon as the lockdown alarm went off, the lunch ladies burst into the gym and instructed them to come to the kitchen area where they positioned the students behind metal tables and cabinets, then got ready to use The Inside Leverage Takeaway disarming technique on anyone who walked into the darkened room. I received similar reports that janitorial staff had gotten students out of restrooms and bunkered in safe areas. The training really worked, and everyone was ready for whatever followed.

What I've learned as a school district superintendent is that whether I actively seek out the type of training offered by Fight Back Nation or not, we absolutely must have a plan in place, and know how to interact with the local police department and SWAT in the event of an incident. Fight Back Nation already had all of the answers, and we didn't need to reinvent any of the wheels that Dave developed through years of on-the-job learning and training. In the final analysis our program is RUN—HIDE—FIGHT, and in that order. Fight

Back Nation taught us the best way to **run**, then the best methods to **hide**. Then, if fight becomes necessary, they taught us how to **fight**. To tell you the truth, the fight is the part our teachers and staff enjoy the most.

Tim Evancich

Chief Operating Officer,

American Preparatory Schools

I cringe a little when I hear the word "empowerment" these days—just because it is so overused and applied to every possible area of learning and training; almost to the extent that it loses its value. I find myself using the word lately, however—and often. I can't think of a word that better describes the transformation of the professionals I work with on a daily basis, and the thousands of students that are receiving the benefits of that transformation as a result of the training they have received from Fight Back Nation.

We have the opportunity to change the mentality of our educators and staff regarding a potential catastrophic event—from one of persistent background fear, to one of "empowerment." This is a gift that we are able to share with them, through the training program that teaches them to be pro active in the event of a catastrophe, exposing and equipping the capable person they truly are. Through the training our teachers and staff gain an incredible amount of confidence—not just in their ability to handle an active shooter situation, but other really stressful conditions, in or out of the school environment. That flowers out into heightened levels of camaraderie and teamwork, in addition to higher levels of confidence in the classroom and their private lives. Victimhood is systemic and insidious. By breaking its hold on us in a very vulnerable area, we tend to release its power over us in all aspects of our lives. That increased level of confidence translates to the students through the teachers, and even during drills when the students are actively thinking about the possibility of tragedy, the confidence and calmness of the teacher transfers to the students.

At our schools, in the event of an actual on-campus active shooter, every student has an assignment, ranging anywhere from calming others, to looking for police officers, to backing up the teacher as soon as she ambushes the shooter with The Inside Leverage Takeaway disarming technique. No one is sitting around waiting to be killed—which has a tremendous psychological benefit to the students. Instead of a classroom filled with victims who could suffer from posttraumatic stress, it is filled with young people with a purpose, who are actively engaged in preserving their lives in an affirmative manner. Beginning discussions and training in this area inherently heightens nerves, and elevates stress levels—but, like staff, the students are so much better off and more confident as a result of active participation rather than cowering in ignorance, fear, and helplessness.

Context is important here; the odds of being killed by a school shooter are astronomically small. Our students are 900 times more likely to be struck by lightening. Nevertheless, lightning strikes, as do school shooters. Therefore, to completely ignore the possibility is unacceptable. Mass shootings are so broadly publicized that they are a part of our daily lives, even though so few of us are ever actually affected by them. Because we feel the weight of the horrible tragedy that would result from a school shooter, we must prepare for it, no matter how remote the chances. We likewise have several fire drills every year, although it has been several decades since a student has died in a school fire. In fact, if we were to portion resources according to where true dangers lie, we would put tremendous resources into preventing the 37,000 traffic accident related deaths each year, 1,600 of which are school children under the age of 15, with an additional 2.35 million are injured or disabled each year—all resulting in costs of $230 billion per year; and that's all in one year in one country. By contrast, a handful of school shootings results in relatively few deaths—but we simply cannot sit back and allow them to occur unanswered. Doing nothing invites crazed cowards to come into our schools and try to massacre our children at will. We will not allow it. We must make it "unproductive," as Dave puts it, and we must stop a school shooter in the beginning of his rampage, and not wait until the end when he has exhausted his ammunition, or simply satisfied his bloodlust.

Whether it is teachers, staff, students or parents—everyone thinks about the school shooter phenomenon, and discusses it from a position of fear and defenselessness. At the time the Sandy Hook Elementary School shooting occurred in December of 2012, in Newtown, Connecticut, every school was thinking about the subject, and what we could do to prevent that type of carnage.

When our schools began looking into what we could do to deal with the possibility of a mass shooter, we were stifled because up until then the general wisdom for school administrators was the use of security technology to fortify the schools. Yet, Sandy Hook had those layered technologies, and they failed to stop the carnage of that horrible day. We needed something more in our schools. I heard Dave Acosta talking about the elementary school teacher who literally blocked her students with her body, and gave her own life, but didn't save a single student by doing so. The incredible bravery and sacrifice of that teacher was negated by the equally astonishing ineffectiveness of her selfless and courageous act—only because she had no idea what she could actually do to be effective. Contrasted with what happened on Flight 93, then in other mass shooter situations where intended victims fought back and foiled the shooters, it became obvious to me that fighting back in the proper manner was the only effective response around which all other security processes must revolve. By giving our teachers and staff all the tools and confidence they need to fight back against an active shooter, we could give them a gift—and change their entire mental process. They would no longer be victims, but capable and confident professionals.

I talked with our directors and we agreed to have Dave Acosta provide school shooter training in a pilot program at our smallest school. On the training day we had around 30 teachers and staff in attendance, and we recognized that they were a diverse group, with differing backgrounds, faith and political beliefs. I wondered if that would influence their receptivity to the training in any way. There was a small group of first and second grade teachers who approached me and told me that they couldn't even think about someone breaking in and murdering their little children, and they were so affected by the subject matter that it would be impossible for them to remain and attend the training. They said they were physically sick and entirely incapable of sitting through such a presentation. Two of the teachers asked to be immediately excused from the training. I looked at them and recognized that the subject of a mass shooter was something that truly haunted them—and for all the appropriate reasons.

I asked the teachers to join the training and to sit with us as long as they possibly could. If they became physically ill, they could leave—but please receive as much of the training as possible, because in fact, it could very well be the only thing that could save their lives and those of their children in the event of a mass shooter in the school. They reluctantly agreed. By the end of the two-hour training with Dave, those two teachers, along with every one of their peers, came up to me and excitedly asked me if we could have Dave back soon for a follow-up training session. They were so enthusiastic, and so empowered from the training—they were visibly changed professional people. For the first time in years their fear had been replaced by knowledge, ability and confidence, and they simply were no longer prisoners of the terror instilled by mass shootings at other schools. The transformation was amazing! I know educators, and they live for that *light bulb moment* when a student suddenly comprehends a concept—as the new information changes their worldview; changes their perspective. I was spellbound as I watched that very thing happen to those 30 educators that day.

Something that I came to perceive following that first training session was that as useful and important as the process and The Inside Leverage Takeaway disarming technique are in empowering teachers and staff in the event of an active shooter in the school, even more important to our educators was the mental shift they experienced—from victim to capable warrior. Just after the training ended I overheard some of the small female teachers saying things like, "I pray something like that never happens at our school, but if it does, I hope I'm the one who takes him down, because I'll kick his ass." I had simply never heard our teachers speak that way before—about anything. They were liberated following the training, in every way. Their empowerment was visibly complete—across the board in every aspect of their lives. I was extremely gratified to see that the decision to have Fight Back Nation train our teachers was so effective.

I paid attention and found that the teachers and staff were talking about the training in the days and weeks that followed. Their sense of camaraderie was heightened. I even saw teachers practicing The Inside Leverage Takeaway disarming technique during their down time together. They would joke around about life's bullies, and how confident they felt in confronting them. This entire process of facing fears had liberated them in ways they hadn't realized they had been held prisoner. They simply were no longer frightened—of anything. It was amazing to witness the transformation.

As a result, we invited Dave and Fight Back Nation to train the educators at all of our schools, and this time I created a feedback form so I could measure the effectiveness of the training. Knowing that our teachers are the best trained and sharpest in the nation, I really wanted their candid feedback, because I knew that they received so much in-service training, that they knew the difference between top-drawer training and space-filler training. I included in the survey questions like, "Was this training an effective use of the limited time and resources that the school and you have?" I also asked, "What was the most effective thing for you? How would you change the course? How would you prioritize the content in the course?" Because of the professional level of our teachers, their feedback was not only extremely positive, but it provided Dave with valuable insights about the presentation of the training, which he modified to fit the suggestions of our educators. Now that over 700 members of our staff have received the Fight Back Nation training—all of them with widely varying backgrounds and political and religious orientations—we are amazed that we have not received a single negative comment about the training; not the presentation, the process, the techniques, or anything. This single fact is, in my mind, the greatest testament to the effectiveness of the training.

Chapter Twelve — The Good Fight

We have trained thousands of educators, tactical and security professionals and corporate clients how to prevent, prepare for and protect against mass shootings. Though these clients come from different backgrounds, the goal is always the same; preserve life during a critical incident. We are all united in the Fight Back mentality.

We believe that anyone can have the fundamental skills to not only survive a mass shooting, but protect those who are around them. We all have a duty to do so. As such, our motto, "Prepare to be the Solution," was developed to ensure that we take personal ownership in our families' and communities' safety. Our goal is to empower you with knowledge and the tools you need to prevail in the face of overwhelming odds.

You are your own First Responder.
Train to be the solution!

Can we prevent 100 percent of mass shootings or active

shooter incidents? No, not a chance; but we can certainly reduce the likelihood of an attack at a given location. For example, the night after the Sutherland Springs mass shooting, I was invited to meet with a local pastor and the elders of his church (about an hour from Sutherland Springs). I spent two hours with him and his group. We created a prevention and response plan for a shooter in their church. At the end of the night, he asked me "What do we do next?" My response was to tell him to email all his parishioners and let them know that he and the elders had spent a few hours meeting with an authority on mass shootings and have come up with a relevant and effective plan to respond to and defeat an active shooter at the church. They will continue to worship God while prepared to defeat evil at the doors! Proclaim openly your preparation and willingness to defend your flock with force.

Being prepared to engage and defeat evil is a huge deterrent to anyone who's intent is to commit a mass shooting. It's about the body count to them. "Gun Free" zones are inviting, soft targets to a shooter. It makes no sense to these murderous psychos to attempt the same thing at a location where people are trained and prepared to fight back.

We need to change our mental approach and our response to an active shooter. All of the dynamics that work in favor of the active shooter also work in our favor if we change our mindset. We need to reject victimhood. In almost every mass shooting in the US, the perpetrators were not trained shooters or tacticians. They were crazy people that made some effort to plan a shooting and had some equipment and ability to carry out the murders. Remember, they have not committed a mass shooting before, even if they have rehearsed it, and they will all experience tunnel vision, because their focus is localized to what is in front of their gun barrel. There is only a vague awareness of the their environment beyond what is directly in front of them.

Jump Up and Fight Back!

If a shooter were targeting your child, would you run, hide or just huddle? None of the above—you certainly would never leave your child behind. You would act! You would attack the person trying to hurt your child. It's in our DNA to protect our kids. You might be a horrible swimmer, terrified of the water. But if your child falls in, you don't stand by, assessing all the reasons why not, weighing the risks of jumping in. You act! So what is the difference here?

I am not involved in any political discussions about why crazy people become mass shooters or what kind of law a legislature thinks it can pass to stop them. While people are taking sides in arguments that so far have done nothing to stop mass shootings, I am actively providing teachers and others with the tools and training they need to repel an attack at that critical moment. The only thing that we can do is make mass shootings in schools and other public places unproductive. The way we do that is by training teachers and others to shut down the attack by fighting back. That is our focus. It is the only effective thing that has worked.

As we have stated before, these shooters are not highly trained assassins. They are nervous, scared cowards. The success of their plan relies 100 percent on whether or not they encounter resistance. They are not prepared for a close, physical counter-attack. They do not have a plan for that nor do they have the training or skills to repel such an attack. Condition Black is where their brains will go when Momma Bear gets them in her grasp.

Our Training is Very Effective

Fight Back Nation was asked to participate in a large scale Active Shooter training scenario near Park City, Utah with the South Summit School District and the Summit County Sheriff's Office. The Summit County SWAT Team would run the law enforcement response training while we focused on working with the educators. We instructed the teachers and staff as we generally do, to prepare them for this interactive, live training scenario and walked them through The Inside Leverage Takeaway disarming technique.

Eddie Wilde is a friend and the team leader on the Summit County SWAT Team. Eddie was playing the part of the mass shooter, moving through the halls with an AR15. When the teachers had all practiced The Inside Leverage Takeaway several times, we had them go into random classrooms and set up for a counter ambush in the event the shooter made his way into their rooms. As far as the training for the responding police officers, Eddie was wandering the halls of the school, randomly firing his AR-15 which was loaded will full blank rounds. What that means is that the sound and the powder burned with each shot was true to life as if a real live .223 round had been fired. Loud and smoky! The intent of being mobile while firing his rifle was to give the arriving officers and teachers a chance to hear what gunfire sounded like in the school, and to pinpoint where the shots were coming from. We had arranged for one of our Fight Back Nation Instructors to hold his orange plastic AR-15 rifle and randomly select classrooms to invade, so teachers could practice The Inside Leverage Takeaway on him.

I was in the hallway near Eddie and watched as he fired off several rounds. After several minutes without being confronted by responding officers, Eddie began to wonder what was going on. I noticed him standing there for a few seconds, then wander from the middle of the wide hallway to one of the classroom doors. It seemed that Eddie made a decision to enter the classroom and was curiously turning the handle, to look inside.

It suddenly occurred to me that this may be one of the classrooms where teachers were waiting for the active shooter (Fight Back Nation trainer) to appear, and my heart jumped as I saw Eddie stick his head into the room and look around to see if anyone was there. Eddie suddenly disappeared and I shouted, "Oh no!" as I ducked under the yellow police tape that separated observers from the participants and stepped toward the classroom. I was only 10 feet from the classroom door when I heard a thud and other noise, then yelling. I could see a pile of people in the room through the narrow glass beside the door, and Eddie's face was ground hard into the industrial carpet on the floor. I jumped forward and yanked open the door. I stepped in and began to remove a couple of small teachers from the dog pile so Eddie could get up.

As we all met in our group at the end of this first scenario, SWAT Team leader, Eddie Wilde shared his experience with the entire group, emotionally recounting as blood trickled down his forehead, his ordeal of being attacked while his eyes were adjusting to the dim light of the room. He recounted how surprised he was that a small female teacher gained inside leverage on him so quickly and flipped him hard to the ground. The sling on his rifle, trapping him in the maneuver. He said, "If I hadn't just gone through it, I would never have believed it was possible for a small teacher to control my weapon so quickly and effectively. I'm glad it happened, because now I know that if I ever have to race to an active shooter situation at one of our schools, our teachers are very capable of keeping everyone as safe as possible until we get there."

From Petrified to Empowered

At one of the school trainings I recently conducted there was a very small teacher hiding as far away behind others in a corner as she could get. I walked over to see what she was doing alone back there, and found that she was crying.

"What's the matter?" I asked her, putting what I hoped

was a comforting arm around her.

"Through her tears she sobbed, "If a gunman came in my room, I couldn't do anything about it. We would all just die. I look at everyone out here practicing the technique and I feel like I'm just not one of them. I just can't do it."

I had my wife Danielle with me at the training, so I asked her to come over and join us. The three of us got off to the side where we weren't in front of a lot of people, and I had Danielle stand in and help us walk through **The Inside Leverage Takeaway** disarming technique. She did this a few times, helping the teacher get used to the movement. After a couple of attempts she was doing it, then she did it again, then again.

Teachers gather around for the demonstration of the Inside Leverage Takeaway before they try it themselves.

"Oh, my gosh," she said. It's really that easy."

"Yeah, it is," I agreed. We only had about ten minutes before the training was over and I could see that the teacher was in very capable hands with Danielle, so I excused myself and left them to practice on their own while I worked with others. When it was time to end I called everyone together into a large circle and asked if there were any final questions.

I told the group how proud I was to see that every one of them had mastered the process and technique that day— even those who were doubtful that they would be able to execute the move. "Every one of you is so full of confidence now. To a person you are able to protect yourselves and your students. If I were to come into your classroom holding this," I said, holding up the orange plastic pistol that we use in training, and before I could complete the sentence that tiny teacher rushed me and instantly threw **The Inside Leverage Takeaway** on me, sending the orange gun flying and me to the floor with a loud thud on the boards.

I was stunned and everyone just stared in disbelief for a second. Then the teachers started to clap, and they all cheered for her. She stood there almost shocked at what she had just done, and started to cry. I could see her newfound confidence overtake her and she straightened up and accepted the applause as she realized that she was no longer a helpless victim. Her singular act of attacking me and disarming me as I brandished the pistol was a testament to everyone there of the effectiveness of the training and the technique. It was also a testament of the transformation and "empowerment" that come with it.

Everyone has the Warrior DNA—the momma bear instinct. Most of us just never learn to tap into it. That's what we teach at Fight Back Nation—how to flip the switch and engage it. School-by-school we are creating a nation of people who refuse to be victims—who will flip the switch and fight back when necessary. Through our training we are making schools hard targets, and we are making mass shootings unproductive. We invite every school, every hospital, and every business and organization to get trained. Every teacher, employee and staff member can be ready for the unthinkable.

Working together, we will be VICTIMS *NO MORE!*

Dave Acosta

Dave Acosta has worked side-by-side with the world's most elite tactical professionals for over 25 years. He started his career in Las Vegas, spending 8 years in specialized units, including six years as the point man on the North Las Vegas SWAT Team and two years as a deputy for the King County Sheriff's Office in Seattle. Dave moved on to become an international tactical instructor as well as a team leader for high-risk protection teams in Iraq, Afghanistan, Africa, Mexico, South and Central America. He has conducted over 1,800 real world tactical missions, and his company, YouTactical, continues to provide protection and tactical training to clients around the globe.

Dave currently trains and works with various law enforcement Tactical Teams from Brazil, training 150 team members a year. These tactical schools include subjects like Urban Counter Ambush, CQB, High-risk Tactical Operations, Hostage Rescue, Tactical Handgun, Tactical M4 (similar), and much more. Dave is considered a national authority on mass shootings/active shooter and has trained thousands of teachers in fight back techniques. He is a guest trainer with the Utah County Sherriff's Office Teacher Academy, one of the most progressive Active Shooter Response Teacher Training programs in the US. Dave is a regular guest on many television and radio programs around the nation, and many other media outlets, where he is used as an expert resource due to his extensive tactical background.

Contact Dave Acosta through his website:
www.FightBackNation.org

Praise for VICTIMS *NO MORE!*

"As a retired Navy SEAL, I spent my entire adult life learning how to place the enemy "On the X," or the point of attack. In September 2007 I found myself on that X in a devastating enemy ambush. Unfortunately, in this day and age, too often, innocent people and school children are finding themselves "on the X" in mass shooting situations. I now teach people how to "Get off the X" from life ambushes, but Dave Acosta is teaching individuals how to Get off the X and Overcome real world mass shooting scenarios. This book will change the mindset in America from being victims and cowering on the X in mass shooting scenarios, to being victors and taking control of the situation. That is what Dave Acosta is teaching. If you are tired of living scared wondering if the next mass shooting incident is going to happen to you or your loved ones, Get off the X and *Buy this book*!"

— Jason "Jay" Redman, Retired Navy SEAL,
New York Times Best-Selling Author of
The Trident and *Overcome*

"Dave and his team did an outstanding job empowering our employees with the skills, mindset, and confidence to react to a potential threat in their space. It's unfortunate in this day and age that we have to take these precautions, but it is completely necessary. I firmly believe this training has increased the safety and security of our students and employees. I look forward to inviting Dave and his team back in the future."

> — Dr. Rick L. Robins, Ed.D., Superintendent, Juab School District, Nephi, Utah

"Dave Acosta is a true American hero and warrior. Whether in his lifelong roles of police officer, SWAT operator, or American representative working with elite units in danger zones like Afghanistan and elsewhere, he has devoted his entire life to saving the lives of others. Dave's greatest fear in life has always been that when predators come, he – or others like him – are not there. This book exists as his effort to help all of those innocent targets of terrorism keep themselves alive until that help does arrive. This is a must-read for everyone in America who ever dares venture forth from his or her home, who enters public places, and especially for those who ever cross the threshold of any school in America. Read it, study it, and remember its lessons. They will save the lives of those who did so, one day."

> — John Giduck, J.D., Ph.D., CHS-V
> Best-Selling Author of: *Terror at Beslan* ✦
> *Shooter Down* ✦ *When Terror Returns*

"Dave Acosta, through his hands-on work, and now this book, is leading a paradigm shift in our culture. From one teacher to one school, and from one employee to one work place, Dave and his team are establishing a FIGHT BACK NATION! Dave champions a mindset of not only survival in and during an active shooter event, but he develops the mind and skills of those thrust into this horror to fight back and to be VICTIMS NO MORE. His work is important. This book is important. This information may help save your life and the life of your family and the life of a student or coworker. It will help you to be a VICTIM NO MORE!"

— Don Goodman, Chief of Police, City of Radford VA, 2008-2019 (Retired); Captain, Blacksburg VA Police Department 1984-2008

"Dave Acosta is changing our country one seminar at a time, by showing teachers and educators how to defend our most precious resource; our children. Defense of others is an act of selfless service without comparison. By teaching the teachers to defend our children, Dave is becoming a leader in selfless service, which is the change our country desperately needs."

— Jeff Kirkham, Retired Master Sergeant, U.S. Army Special Forces, Best-selling author of *Black Autumn* ◆ *Black Autumn "Conquistadors"* ◆ *Black Autumn "The Last Air Force One"* ◆ *Black Autumn "Travelers"* ◆ *Combat Field Leaders Guide*

Made in the USA
Middletown, DE
03 December 2020

25179110R00089